eBay Millionaire

or Bust

Hidden Strategies That

Maximize Profits and Create Wealth

Corey Kossack

Published 2006 by Entrepreneur Education Group LLC, 5377 N. Ventana Vista Rd., Tucson, AZ 85750.

Edited by Nancy McCurry

Printed in the United States of America

Acknowledgement

First and foremost, I would like to thank my business partners, Kevin Kossack and Stephanie Kossack, who have been instrumental to the success of my companies. Your creativity, hard work and passion have propelled me to where I am today.

Second, I would like to thank Alan H. Kossack of Kossack Investment Planning in Tucson, Arizona for your guidance in planning a successful financial future for me and those who follow in my footsteps.

I thank Casey Kossack for being a great brother and always having an outstanding attitude.

I thank Jules Nayfack for teaching me the power of positive thinking.

Thank you to the rest of my family and close friends who have always supported me in everything that I have done.

Thank you to the wonderful, friendly staff at eBay. I have enjoyed working with each one of you and look forward to a bright future together. I firmly believe that without eBay, Koss DVD would not be what it is today.

Thank you to Sethmatics Inc. for their technical contributions to my companies.

Last of all, I would like to thank Peter J. Burns III, President of the College of Entrepreneurship, who taught me to dream big and "go for it". You have inspired me to do the impossible and ignore those who say it can't be done.

Table of Contents

PART A: PROFITABILITY

PART B: PRODUCT ACQUISITION AND PRICING

INTRODUCTION

Will you be an eBay millionaire? Or will you be a "successful" PowerSeller who sells thousands or millions of dollars worth of products every year, but actually makes a lot less money than you think? Believe it or not, this is happening to eBay sellers today, and some of them may not even realize this is happening to them...yet.

The world of eBay is an exciting one, where 200 million users worldwide gather to buy and sell the widest selection of merchandise on the web today. For sellers, eBay is a dream come true. No matter how big or small your business, eBay allows sellers to have their products seen by millions, and even encourages buyers to compete for the privilege of purchasing your product.

While eBay can be an exciting and profitable environment to sell in, it can also be a very challenging one. To be successful on eBay, you must have a detailed understanding of your costs of doing business and your risks of listing certain items for sale, keep conversion rates high (the ratio of items that are sold vs. the items that do not sell), provide outstanding customer service and have listing formats and prices that appeal to your customers. This book was written to teach you how to do all of these things, with an emphasis on cost and risk management.

Quite possibly the most important part of running your eBay business will be taking the time to understand what your profit margins really are, to allow yourself to cut losses in the areas that are hurting your profitability, and build upon the areas that are adding value to your bottom line.

Don't forget that selling on eBay is a business. Like any business, your goal is to increase profits, not simply to increase sales. EBay's PowerSeller program is set up in a way to reward sellers for their monthly gross sales volume. The PowerSeller levels are as follows:

Bronze	$1,000
Silver	$3,000
Gold	$10,000
Platinum	$25,000
Titanium	$150,000

While becoming a platinum or titanium PowerSeller can be a great thing and can lead to making a very good living on eBay, this designation seems to lead some sellers astray. Instead of focusing on improving their bottom line, many sellers focus on improving their gross sales to move up the ranks and become one of the "elite" and "successful" PowerSellers.

I recently lectured at eBay's annual convention, "eBay Live", as part of a panel of four top sellers who were selected to share their stories of success with an audience of 1400 PowerSellers. As eBay introduced each one of us, boasting of our millions of dollars in annual gross revenue, I could tell what the audience was thinking. "Wow, these guys are millionaires, if I can find out what they did to sell so many items I can be a millionaire too!" The truth is eBay did not reveal the actual profitability of any of our companies (and neither did any of the sellers); eBay simply showcased the dollar amount of sales that each of us had achieved in the last year. For all the audience knew, my company had a net profit of $1,000,000 last year. Or maybe my company had a negative net profit of $100,000 last year. I could have sold every single one of my products at $5 below my cost and lost money on every sale, and no one would know. I would still have been celebrated as a successful top seller on eBay, even though in reality my business could have been a miserable failure (in truth my business was quite successful, but my point is still a valid one). In fact, eBay has no idea how profitable any of its top sellers are. But somehow this very important detail gets overlooked, and the new and emerging sellers leave the room with the assumption that the experts on the panel are all millionaires, and that the key to profitability on eBay lies within the ability to grow your sales volume to the titanium level and beyond.

Earlier this year there was an article published in the business section of our city's newspaper about me and my company. The article was meant to show how amazing it was that someone could sell so much on eBay, and went on to explain how professional consultants were projecting that my business would turn into a "multi-million dollar company in short order". All of a sudden I noticed my friends coming up to me saying, "I figured you were making good money, but I didn't realize you were making THAT much money!" I even had a friend who told me a story about an experience he had while he was at work which I found to be absolutely hilarious. As he was sitting in the office, one of his colleagues leaned over and said:

"Hey did you hear about that guy who is making millions selling stuff on eBay?"
"Wait, are you talking about Corey Kossack?"
"Yeah, you know him?!"
"Yeah, he's my good friend."
"You know I had the same idea, I'm going to do the same thing and be a millionaire too."

The story was so amusing because this person's assumptions were based on the sales figures outlined in the article which really have very little to do with profitability. However, perception is everything, and the average person will not think twice before assuming that millions in sales revenue actually equals millions in profits. Understanding that these two do not always go hand in hand will be your first step to starting and growing your own successful eBay business.

At this point you are probably thinking to yourself, "How can someone sell millions of products on eBay and lose money?" I will go into great detail about this in Chapter 2 on profitability, but for now just keep in mind a few things. There are many costs to selling on eBay, some obvious and some that are a bit hidden. As a seller, if you do not fully understand every detail of these costs, you can easily have a skewed perception of the profits that you are making on eBay. For many sellers, between keeping track of these costs, having thousands of dollars tied up in inventory, dealing with non-paying bidders and just simply managing the day-to-day operations of their business, selling on eBay can leave sellers lost and confused as to how profitable their business really is. And remember, just because you bought an item for $8 and sold it on eBay for $9, that doesn't necessarily mean you actually turned a profit.

The first part of this book will cover the profitability of an eBay business. You will learn to analyze all costs associated with selling on eBay and how those costs impact the overall success of your business. Next you will discover the importance of monitoring unsold listings to maximize profits. With your new understanding of the effect of unsold listings on profitability, you will be introduced to a patent-pending program called ProfitBuilder Software that will save your business thousands of dollars. The ProfitBuilder Software will calculate profit margins for you, and analyze the risk of listing certain items for sale using different pricing strategies and listing features. Using this information, ProfitBuilder will help you determine which listing strategies yield the most profit for your company, and will also help you identify which products to sell. Next, you will be exposed to a wide-range of hidden tips and tricks that cut costs and boost profitability. These tips include establishing banking relationships that transform sales revenue into extra profits, strategies that reduce the cost of packaging materials and postage, methods to alter your business processes to save money and much more.

Once you have a better understanding of how to maximize the profitability of your company, PART B of this book will share information regarding product acquisition and pricing. You will learn about the supply chain of products and what your role as an eBay business will be in the chain. You will be taught how to negotiate with suppliers to get the best prices and terms on quality products to sell. You will then discover how to select products to sell and determine the best price at which to list these items on eBay.

PART C of this book will reveal additional tips for running your eBay business related to customer service, shipping and handling, and how to keep costs low during start-up and growth. You will use these strategies to keep eBay customers coming back while structuring costs in a way that enables the growth of your company.

Finally, PART D will show you how to generate the largest return from your eBay business using investing and wealth building strategies. You will learn how to structure your business legally with the government to protect your assets and take full advantage of legal tax breaks given to small businesses. Now that you know how to structure your business, you will find out how to maximize profits using tax loopholes and business deductions to reduce the amount of tax you owe the government. Next you will discover how to transfer these tax savings into investments that build your net worth. Finally, all of this information will be tied together to put you on the road to becoming the next eBay Millionaire!

PART A:

PROFITABILITY

1

Understanding Your Profit Margins

If you are selling on eBay you are running a business. Business is about delivering value to your customers in hopes that one day your business will become profitable. Understanding your profit margins is essential to running your eBay business effectively. If you purchase an item from a supplier for $8, and sell it for $9, you might think that your net profit margin is $1. Actually this is not the case. Did you think about eBay fees, PayPal fees, cost of postage, labor costs, email support, or the cost of packaging materials? Some of these costs are easily quantifiable, and others are much more difficult to measure, so you need to leave a little bit of extra padding to make sure you're achieving your goals for profitability when selling on eBay. Before we get too deep into this issue, I will give you a break down of eBay and PayPal's fee structures so that we can get a better understanding of what we are talking about.

There is a great deal of information to digest in this chapter including a bunch of numbers. Don't worry if you feel overwhelmed by the numbers or the examples, the key here is to familiarize yourself with eBay's fee policies and how they can impact the profitability of your company. Think of this chapter as a resource guide for your continuing education on how to run an eBay business. Now let's look at eBay's fee policies and some examples.

EBay Insertion Fees

EBay charges a fee for listing the item on the site for a period of time ranging from 3-10 days (a 10-day listing carries an extra $0.40 fee). The insertion fee is based on the value of the "starting bid" or "Fixed Price" of the item, depending on which listing format you choose (auction or Fixed Price). For example, a listing with a starting bid or Fixed Price value of $10.00-$24.99 would have an insertion fee of $0.60. The following chart shows you the breakdown for fees.

EBay Insertion Fee Chart

Listing Price	Fee
$0.01-$0.99	$0.20
$1.00-$9.99	$0.35
$10.00-$24.99	$0.60

Listing Price	Fee
$25.00-$49.99	$1.20
$50.00-$199.99	$2.40
$200.00-$499.99	$3.60
$500.00 and above	$4.80

EBay Final Value Fees

EBay also charges the seller a final value fee when the item sells. Upon closing of your auction or Fixed Price listing, a fee is charged based on the sales price of the item. The following chart breaks down how this fee structure works.

EBay Final Value Fee Chart

Sales Price	Fee
Item not sold	no fee
$0.01-$25.00	5.25% of sales price
$25.01-$1,000.00	5.25% of first $25 ($1.31) + 3.0% of remaining amount
$1,000.01 and above	5.25% of first $25 ($1.31) + 3.0% of amount between $25.01-$1,000.00 ($29.25) + 1.5% of remaining amount

Sellers are charged 5.25% of the sales price for an item that has a selling price of $25 or less. If the value of the item is greater than $25, the seller is charged 5.25% for the first $25, then 3.0% on the remaining amount of the sales price up to $1000. For example, if the sales price was $45, the seller would be charged 5.25% of the first $25 ($1.31) and 3.0% of the $20 that is remaining ($0.60). Together the total final value fee would be $1.91 for an item that sells for $45. If the sales price is above $1,000, the same rule will apply, but the remaining amount above $1,000 will only carry a fee of 1.5%.

EBay Buy It Now Fees

EBay charges sellers a fee when they elect to add the Buy It Now option to an auction-style listing. The Buy It Now option allows buyers to end the auction early by opting to purchase the item immediately at a price specified by the seller. If a buyer chooses to Buy It Now, the auction will end instantly and no other buyers can bid. The fee is based on the value of the Buy It Now price specified by the seller. This fee does not apply to Fixed Price or Store Inventory Format listings.

EBay Buy It Now Fee Chart

Buy It Now Price	Fee
$0.01-$9.99	$0.05
$10.00-$24.99	$0.10

Buy It Now Price	Fee
$25.00-$49.99	$0.20
$50.00 and above	$0.25

EBay Feature Fees

EBay offers a number of listing upgrades to enhance the look, feel and visibility of your item listing. By enhancing your listing with additional features, you can potentially create more interest in your item. For more information on each individual type of feature, please visit www.ebay.com

Feature	Fee
Gallery picture	$0.35
Scheduled Listing	$0.10
Bold:	$1.00
Gift	$0.25
Value Pack	$0.65
Gallery Featured	$19.95
Subtitle	$0.50
Border	$3.00
Highlight	$5.00

10-Day Duration	$0.40
Listing Designer	$0.10
Homepage Featured	$39.95
Featured Plus	$19.95
List in 2 Categories	(doubles most fees)

PayPal Fees

PayPal charges fees to sellers based on the amount of business they transact with PayPal each month. Keep in mind that this total is the total dollar amount of your transaction, which includes the sales price, shipping and handling, insurance or any additional services that the customer pays extra for. The fees vary from 1.9%-2.9% depending on your volume, and have an additional $0.30 charge per transaction, no matter what volume level you are at. Here is how it breaks down:

Monthly Volume	Fee
Less than $3,000	2.9% + $0.30
$3,000-$10,000	2.5% + $0.30
$10,000-$100,000	2.2% + $0.30
$100,000 or more	1.9% + $0.30

Postage Rates

Postage rates can be a little tricky to figure out ahead of time, but depending on the types of products you are selling, you may be able to standardize this a little bit. Postage rates are based on the weight and shipping destination of the package. Please check www.usps.com or www.ups.com to calculate postage rates for your items.

Listing Formats: Auction, Fixed Price and Store Inventory

EBay allows you to choose one of three different listing formats when you list your item for sale. Each format has its advantages and drawbacks. Here's a brief introduction to each format right now, and you will learn great detail about the benefits of each type of format as you continue on through the book.

Auctions

The auction format is the most traditional listing format on eBay. Using this format, buyers will have a chance to bid on your item and compete to win the auction at a price that is determined completely by how high the buyers bid the item up. With the auction format, you will be given the option to add a Buy It Now price for an additional fee. This will allow bidders to purchase the item instantly at a price that you specify. If a buyer chooses to buy the item now, the auction will end immediately and no other buyers will have a chance to bid. An auction-style listing will be visible to buyers when they search for an item on www.ebay.com and when they are browsing through product categories.

Fixed Price

You can also choose to list your item using the Fixed Price format. With Fixed Price, you only specify a Buy It Now price; there is no bidding like there is with the auction format. There is no additional Buy It Now fee for this format, as the Buy It Now feature is already included in your cost to list the item as a Fixed Price listing. A Fixed Price listing will be visible to buyers when they search for an item on www.ebay.com and when they are browsing through product categories.

Store Inventory Format (SIF)

The last option you have is the Store Inventory Format. Store inventory listings will not usually show up in general search results on www.ebay.com, but are visible when buyers are browsing through your eBay store and when other special conditions apply. This format has much cheaper insertion fees, but is much less visible to customers than the auction and Fixed Price formats.

Now that we have covered some of the basics, let's start with some examples. I will cover specific benefits and tips related to each of the individual fees and how you can use these rules to your advantage in chapter 4: Hidden tips and tricks to cut costs and boost your profitability. Remember, you don't need to memorize these numbers or take it all in at once. Each example has been included to show you how different listing options can impact the profitability of your listing.

Each example will show you the listing format, price you are listing the item for, your cost of goods, cost of postage, and any eBay and PayPal fees that apply. Keep your eye out for differences in the listing options chosen for different examples. You will see some examples using the Fixed Price format and some using the auction format. You will also see examples using listing upgrades like the gallery feature and examples that do not have any listing features selected. Watch how each one of these little decisions changes the net profit for the item. I will point out important numbers in each example as we go through them. Now for the examples:

Profitability examples using the Fixed Price Format:

Example #1

Listing format on eBay: Fixed Price

Buy It Now Price:	$9.00
Shipping and handling charged to customer:	$2.00
Total price charged to customer:	$11.00
Cost of goods from supplier:	$8.00
Cost of postage:	$1.52
Cost of packaging materials:	$0.25

EBay feature fees: none

PayPal rate: 2.9% + $0.30 (based on less than $3,000/month sales volume)

Fees for this example:

EBay insertion fee:	$0.35
EBay Final Value fee:	$0.47
PayPal fee:	$0.62
Total fees:	$1.44

Profitability for this example:

Total amount charged to customer:	$11.00
Cost of goods from supplier:	$8.00
Total fees:	$1.44
Cost of postage:	$1.52
Cost of packaging materials:	$0.25
Net Profit:	**-$0.21**

Let's think about this for a minute. You bought the item for $8.00. You sold the item for $9.00. You more than covered the cost of your postage as your cost of postage and packaging materials was $1.77 and you charged the customer $2.00 for it, and yet you still lost money on the sale. EBay fees account for a lot more of your profit than you may think, so you need to find products that are profitable enough to allow you to succeed on eBay. You might be saying to yourself, "That's terrible, the fees are too high, I am just going to open my own website and do it without eBay." If this is what you are thinking, I strongly urge you to reconsider. EBay has 200 million users. If eBay was a country, it would have one of the largest populations in the world; it is highly unlikely you will have that kind of customer base at your fingertips if you take your business completely off of eBay. In addition, driving traffic to your own website is a lot more difficult and expensive than you might imagine. Think of your eBay fees as the cost of marketing for your business. In my experience, eBay is the absolute best deal on the Internet in terms of the cost to acquire a customer that will view and purchase an item. Without eBay, I honestly don't know if my business would have been successful at all. So, now that we know we still want to sell on eBay, even though much of our profit has to be used to pay for fees, let's figure out how we can actually turn this into a profitable business.

Example #2

Listing format on eBay: Fixed Price

Buy It Now Price:	$38.00
Shipping and handling charged to customer:	$5.00
Total price charged to customer:	$43.00
Cost of goods from supplier:	$30.00
Cost of postage:	$3.00
Cost of packaging materials:	$0.40
EBay feature fees: gallery picture	$0.35
scheduled listing	$0.10

PayPal rate: 2.9% + $0.30 (based on less than $3,000/month sales volume)

Fees for this example:

EBay insertion fee:	$1.20
EBay feature fees:	$0.45
EBay Final Value fee:	$1.70
PayPal fee:	$1.55
Total fees:	$4.90

Profitability for this example:

Total amount charged to customer:	$43.00
Cost of goods from supplier:	$30.00
Total fees:	$4.90
Cost of postage:	$3.00
Cost of packaging materials:	$0.40
Net Profit:	**$4.70**

In this example, we sold our product for $8 above our cost, made an additional $1.60 on the shipping and handling (our cost of postage and materials was only $3.40 and we charged the customer $5.00) which left us with a net profit of $4.70 because of our fees.

Example #3

Listing format on eBay: Fixed Price

Buy It Now Price:	$58.00
Shipping and handling charged to customer:	$5.00
Total price charged to customer:	$63.00
Cost of goods from supplier:	$50.00
Cost of postage:	$3.00
Cost of packaging materials:	$0.40
EBay feature fees: gallery picture	$0.35
scheduled listing	$0.10

PayPal rate: 2.9% + $0.30 (based on less than $3,000/month sales volume)

Fees for this example:

EBay insertion fee:	$2.40
EBay feature fees:	$0.45
EBay Final Value fee:	$2.30
PayPal fee:	$2.13
Total fees:	$7.28

You will notice that the only major difference between this example and the previous is that the sales price is $20 higher. But with this price increase, your fees increased $2.38, from $4.90 to $7.28, due in large part to the increased insertion fee of listing the item for more than $49.99.

Profitability for this example:

Total amount charged to customer: $63.00

Cost of goods from supplier: $50.00

Total fees: $7.28

Cost of postage: $3.00

Cost of packaging materials: $0.40

Net Profit: **$2.32**

Again, we are selling our item for $8 above our cost and making an additional $1.60 on the shipping and handling, but this time our profit margin has been reduced to $2.32, due to the increase of our insertion and final value fees.

Keep in mind that none of these examples have taken into consideration your hidden costs. How much is it costing you to answer emails to all of your buyers? What about the cost of managing your inventory and shipping and receiving? Does your supplier charge you shipping and handling to deliver goods to your location?

Auctions

Want to try your luck selling the item using the auction format? Auctions can be a tricky deal. You never know how many buyers will be interested in your product at any given time, and one buyer's bidding behavior may be completely different than the behavior of another buyer. Occasionally you may find two buyers who will find themselves in a bidding war, willing to pay any price just to win, while other times an increase of $0.50 in the current bidding price is enough to drive some buyers to give up and purchase from someone else.

There are a number of ways to run an auction. You can have a bid with a Buy It Now option, which can be slightly above the price of the starting bid, or quite a bit higher. You can also run the auction with a starting bid and no Buy It Now option. You can start the bid at a price you are comfortable with, which may be the price that would allow you to "break-even" on the sale, or maybe satisfy the minimum amount of profit you are willing to accept to make the auction worth your while. A riskier, but sometimes profitable option that many sellers use is to start their auction at a penny, relying on high demand for the item to drive buyers to bid the item up to a level beyond the seller's cost. Take extreme caution when using this approach which will be discussed in more detail later. For now, let's take a look at some examples to see how these different auction methods can impact our profitability.

Profitability Examples Using the Auction Format

Example #4

Listing format on eBay: Auction

Starting Bid:	$8.00
Buy It Now Price:	$9.00
Shipping and handling charged to customer:	<u>$5.00</u>
Total price charged to customer: (assuming item is purchased at Buy It Now price)	$14.00
Cost of goods from supplier:	$8.00
Cost of postage:	$1.52
Cost of packaging materials:	$0.25

EBay feature fees: none

PayPal rate: 2.9% + $0.30 (based on less than $3,000/month sales volume)

Fees for this example:

EBay insertion fee:	$0.35
EBay Buy It Now fee:	$0.05
EBay Final Value fee:	$0.47
PayPal fee:	$0.71
Total fees:	$1.58

Profitability for this example:

Total amount charged to customer:	$14.00
Cost of goods from supplier:	$8.00
Total fees:	$1.58
Cost of postage:	$1.52
Cost of packaging materials:	$0.25
Net Profit:	**$2.65**

Using this type of listing strategy as opposed to Fixed Price, you are paying an additional $0.05 to have the Buy It Now available at $9.00. Also keep in mind, a buyer could easily place a bid at $8.00 and win, but for the purposes of this example we have assumed that the buyer has chosen to Buy It

Now for $9.00. If you think that buyers are pretty likely to opt for the Buy It Now instead of bidding, you may consider turning this into a Fixed Price listing at $9.00 and save yourself the extra $0.05 you are paying to have the Buy It Now option on the auction. I know we are only talking about a nickel, but a nickel for thousands of items equals thousands of dollars in additional profit.

Example #5

Listing format on eBay: Auction

Starting Bid:	$37.00
Buy It Now Price:	$38.00
Shipping and handling charged to customer:	<u>$5.00</u>
Total price charged to customer: (assuming item is purchased at Buy It Now price)	$43.00
Cost of goods from supplier:	$30.00
Cost of postage:	$3.00
Cost of packaging materials:	$0.40

EBay feature fees: none

PayPal rate: 2.9% + $0.30 (based on less than $3,000/month sales volume)

Fees for this example:

EBay insertion fee:	$1.20
EBay Buy It Now fee:	$0.20
EBay Final Value fee:	$1.70
PayPal fee:	$1.55
Total fees:	$4.65

Profitability for this example:

Total amount charged to customer:	$43.00
Cost of goods from supplier:	$30.00
Total fees:	$4.65
Cost of postage:	$3.00
Cost of packaging materials:	$0.40
Net Profit:	**$4.95**

Compare this example to example #4 and notice how our fees have increased significantly. The total fees for example #4 were $1.58 but in this example were $4.65. Our fees are so much higher because of the value of the item. Our insertion fees are higher because our starting bid is $37.00, and our Buy It Now fee has increased to $0.20 since we have set the Buy It Now price at $38.00. In addition, our Final Value and PayPal fees have increased because of the final selling price of the item.

Example #6 - Auction without Buy It Now option

Listing format on eBay: Auction

Starting Bid: $30.00

Final Bid (the closing price that your buyers bid the item up to): $40.00

Shipping and handling charged to customer: $5.00

Total price charged to customer: $45.00

Cost of goods from supplier: $30.00

Cost of postage: $3.00

Cost of packaging materials: $0.40

EBay feature fees: none

PayPal rate: 2.9% + $0.30 (based on less than $3,000/month sales volume)

Fees for this example:

EBay insertion fee: $1.20

EBay Final Value fee: $1.76

PayPal fee: $1.61

Total fees: $4.57

Profitability for this example:

Total amount charged to customer:	$45.00
Cost of goods from supplier:	$30.00
Total fees:	$4.57
Cost of postage:	$3.00
Cost of packaging materials:	$0.40
Net Profit:	**$7.03**

In this example, our profits skyrocketed because the buyers bid up the item beyond what the expected Buy It Now price would have been. Keep in mind in this scenario a buyer could have bid at $30 and won, in which case your profitability would have decreased by $9.41, leaving you with a loss of $2.38. This example illustrates the potential risk and reward of using the auction format.

Example #7 - Starting bid of one penny

Listing format on eBay: Auction

Starting Bid:	$0.01
Final Bid (the closing price that your buyers bid the item up to):	$40.00
Shipping and handling charged to customer:	<u>$5.00</u>
Total price charged to customer:	$45.00
Cost of goods from supplier:	$30.00
Cost of postage:	$3.00
Cost of packaging materials:	$0.40

EBay feature fees: none

PayPal rate: 2.9% + $0.30 (based on less than $3,000/month sales volume)

Fees for this example:

EBay insertion fee:	$0.20
EBay Final Value fee:	$1.76
PayPal fee:	<u>$1.61</u>
Total fees:	$3.57

Profitability for this example:

Total amount charged to customer:	$45.00
Cost of goods from supplier:	$30.00
Total fees:	$3.57
Cost of postage:	$3.00
Cost of packaging materials:	<u>$0.40</u>
Net Profit:	**$8.03**

In this example, we have increased our profitability over the previous example because we had the advantage of a lower insertion fee by starting our auction at one penny. However, we are assuming much additional risk because there is a small chance that the item could sell for one penny. To fully understand this risk, let's do an example in which the item sells at the starting bid of one penny. Hopefully this will not happen to you because you would have researched this item properly to know that there is sufficient demand to cause buyers to bid up the auction to a satisfactory level, but for the purposes of illustration let's imagine that your item sells for only one penny.

Example #8 - Complete disaster - item sells for one penny

Listing format on eBay: Auction

Starting Bid:	$0.01
Final Bid (the closing price that your buyers bid the item up to):	$0.01
Shipping and handling charged to customer:	$5.00
Total price charged to customer:	$5.01
Cost of goods from supplier:	$30.00
Cost of postage:	$3.00
Cost of packaging materials:	$0.40

EBay feature fees: none

PayPal rate: 2.9% + $0.30 (based on less than $3,000/month sales volume)

Fees for this example:

EBay insertion fee:	$0.20
EBay Final Value fee:	$0.00
PayPal fee:	$0.45
Total fees:	$0.65

Profitability for this example:

Total amount charged to customer:	$5.01
Cost of goods from supplier:	$30.00
Total fees:	$0.65
Cost of postage:	$3.00
Cost of packaging materials:	$0.40
Net Profit:	**$-29.04**

Ok, so this example is a little extreme, but it proves its point nonetheless. This probably won't happen to your auction but it can. Starting your bid at one penny can potentially attract a lot of attention from buyers, drive them to look at other items in your store, and possibly motivate them to become engaged in the bidding process and bid your item up to a level that is higher than what you might expect for a standard Buy It Now price, but it certainly carries its risks. Please research your item properly before you test this listing tactic out.

Using The Store Inventory Format

Listing your item using the Store Inventory Format is an interesting alternative to the traditional auction or Fixed Price listings. Insertion fees for store inventory listings are significantly cheaper than running an auction or Fixed Price listing, but have far less exposure on www.eBay.com. Selling an item using the Store Inventory Format is much less risky than listing with auction or Fixed Price because the insertion fees are so low, but you also can be fairly certain that your item will take much longer to sell than if it was listed with auction or Fixed Price. Recent reports by eBay state that the average store inventory listing takes up to 14 times longer to sell than an auction or Fixed Price listing. In addition, the report released that items in certain media categories tend to stay on the site up to 40 times longer than an auction or Fixed Price listing. The fees for store inventory listings are as follows:

Store Inventory Format Insertion Fees

Listing Price	Fee
$0.01-$24.99	$0.05/30 days
$25.00 and above	$0.10/30 days

You can either list your item for 30 days only, or you can choose to have a listing that is "Good Till' Cancelled". Good Till' Cancelled listings will automatically be re-listed every 30 days until the item either sells or you decide to cancel the listing. EBay will charge you per month to run this listing, no matter the listing price. This can provide a huge savings over auction or fixed, given that insertion fees for those can run up to

$4.80 for a 7-day listing. However, store inventory listings have much higher Final Value fees than eBay's regular Final Value fees. I have listed these fees below.

Store Inventory Format Final Value Fees

Sales Price	Fee
$0.01-$25.00	10.00% of sales price
$25.01-$100.00	10.00% of first $25 ($2.50) + 7.0% of remaining amount
$100.00-$1,000.00	10.00% of first $25 ($2.50) + 7.0% of amount between $25.01-$100.00 ($5.25) + 5.0% of remaining amount
$1,000.01 and above	10.00% of first $25 ($2.50) + 7.0% of amount between $25.01-$100.00 ($5.25) + 5.0% of amount between $100.01-$1,000.00 ($45.00) + 3.0% of remaining amount

This fee structure works similarly to eBay's fee structure for auction and Fixed Price but the rates are much higher. Even though the Final Value fees are much higher than fixed or auction, the smaller amount of risk can make store inventory listings an appealing option. In addition, profitability for store inventory items can be similar to that of fixed and auction listings depending on the listing price. The closer your listing price is to dropping down to the next lowest price break of insertion fees, the larger your savings will be over auction or Fixed Price. For example, you will save more money in fees when your listing price is $51 than you would at $49 (compared to auction or Fixed Price), since normal insertion fees for auction and fixed raise from $1.20 to $2.40 when the price rises above $49.99. With store inventory the fee is only $0.10 for any item priced at $25.00 or above. I will give a number of examples shortly to demonstrate the difference in profitability of store inventory listings at various levels.

When To Use The Store Inventory Listing Format

One very successful tactic that you can use as a seller is to offer complementary products to your buyers. For example, let's say that your eBay store is dedicated to selling IPODs and IPOD accessories. Your listings for IPODs have very high conversion rates and are making strong enough profits, but your IPOD accessories are suffering. You still get a significant number of sales on your IPOD accessories, but your conversion rates are fairly low, and the unsold listings are hurting your profitability. You also notice that a considerable amount of your sales for accessories come from buyers who are purchasing an IPOD from you at the same time. If this is the case, this means it doesn't matter much that your accessories are showing up in eBay search results, because most likely the buyer is searching or browsing through your eBay store for the accessories to go with the IPOD they are purchasing from you. So you decide to move your accessories (or at least some of them) to a Store Inventory Format. You still see similar sales numbers with the accessories, or maybe slightly lower numbers, but you have eliminated the cost of those unsold listings that were killing your profitability.

Deciding whether or not to move a number of your listings to store inventory is a tough question to answer, but it is important to remember that store inventory listings are much less risky than running an auction or Fixed Price listing. With store inventory listings you essentially eliminate the cost of unsold listings. With standard fixed or auction listings you run the risk of having your item not sell in the first week or two and costing you additional fees (we will talk about how critical this issue is in chapter 2). But with store inventory the only risk you have is the $0.05 or $0.10 every month to have your listing up for sale. While this is a definite plus, we still have to examine the downside of using this listing method.

1) Far less exposure on www.eBay.com

When a buyer goes to www.eBay.com and types in a search for the item they are looking for, the search results will pull up all auction and Fixed Price listings that match the buyer's search, but NOT store inventory listings. However, if there are less than 20 search results that match the buyer's request, store inventory listings will be displayed at the bottom of the page. If you are selling in the more competitive categories, most likely there will be more than 20 search results for your item, and your store inventory listing will not show up. But, if you are competing in more of a niche market, this may work for you.

2) If you rely too heavily on store inventory, you are ignoring eBay's core customers

Keep in mind that the rules for how store inventory listings are displayed on www.eBay.com can change at any time, as eBay has changed their policy on this numerous times. Earlier this year eBay decided to display all store inventory listings at the bottom of the search results page, no matter how many results came up in a buyer's search. Sellers who relied heavily on store inventory listings were pleased with this move on eBay's part, but eBay quickly rolled back this policy as traffic and sales numbers on the site took a quick tumble. Buyers were exiting the site quicker than before and purchasing less often. EBay gathered from this data that the site was becoming too confusing, with too many hundreds of search results, and not enough auctions. EBay built its foundation on providing a platform for buyers to bid on auctions, not simply to be just another shopping comparison site. EBay will be much more cautious in the future to greatly increase the exposure of store inventory listings on the core site, so don't expect store inventory listings to gain too much additional exposure any time in the near future.

3) Do you have to hold the item in inventory, and are you paying interest to finance your inventory?

Possibly the biggest downside of selling with the Store Inventory Format is that most items will take much longer to sell. To give you the basic idea, I'll give an example from my own eBay business. This last month, my store inventory listings accounted for about 15% of the items I had up for sale, but only 2.5% of my sales for the month actually came from store inventory listings. Of course, every eBay business is different, but in most cases store inventory moves much slower than a regular listing would.

So this brings up the question: are you holding these items in inventory or are you having your supplier ship the item to your customers directly, without any up front costs on your part prior to the sale? If you are holding it in inventory there are a few things you need to think about. Is it critical to your business that you have constant cash rolling in so you can pay your bills? Or are you comfortably financed to the point that you don't mind having money tied up for a while? If you need the cash constantly rolling in, store inventory is likely not the way to go.

The other issue that many sellers run into is financing their inventory. If you haven't built up equity in your company to finance the inventory you are holding, you are likely utilizing credit from your supplier, or possibly a credit line from a bank. In either case you may owe interest for the products that you are purchasing on credit depending on what your terms are. Most suppliers will give a 30-day grace period before invoices are due and will charge high interest rates thereafter. Banks are a little different. If you are using a credit card issued to your business by a bank, you will also have the grace period. However, if you are using a line of credit extended to you by the bank, you will pay interest immediately, which is usually around 7-9% annually, but can vary depending upon your arrangement with the bank. If this is the model you are using, you need to account for the interest being paid out when you are examining your profit margins. Here is an example of how interest can affect your overall profitability.

- Assume an 8% annual interest rate (0.66% monthly)
- This means for every $100 that is financed by credit, you will pay 66 cents in interest per month.

This sounds like nothing, but if you were financing $100,000 of inventory (assuming you could get that large a credit line from the bank), you would pay $660 a month in interest to the bank. Depending on what kind of profit margins you are expecting from your inventory that might be taking a while to sell, this isn't necessarily enough of an expense to keep you from financing your inventory, but keep in mind this is an added expense you may not have been thinking about. Take a hard look at your inventory and what it's worth to you, and from there you can decide if you want to sell your item in store inventory, auction, Fixed Price or get rid of the item altogether.

Profitability Examples Using The Store Inventory Format

Example #9

Listing format on eBay: Store Inventory Format

Buy It Now Price:	$49.00
Shipping and handling charged to customer:	$5.00
Total price charged to customer:	$54.00
Cost of goods from supplier:	$40.00
Cost of postage:	$3.00
Cost of packaging materials:	$0.40

EBay feature fees: none

PayPal rate: 2.9% + $0.30 (based on less than $3,000/month sales volume)

Fees for this example:

If Store Inventory Format:		If Fixed Price format:	
EBay insertion fee:	$0.10	EBay insertion fee:	$1.20
EBay Final Value fee:	$4.18	EBay Final Value fee:	$2.03
PayPal fee:	$1.87	PayPal fee:	$1.87
Total fees:	$6.15	Total fees:	$5.10

Profitability for this example:

If Store Inventory Format:		If Fixed Price format:	
Amount charged:	$54.00	Amount charged:	$54.00
Cost of goods from supplier:	$40.00	Cost of goods:	$40.00
Total fees:	$6.15	Total fees:	$5.10
Cost of postage:	$3.00	Cost of postage:	$3.00
Cost of packaging:	$0.40	Cost of packaging:	$0.40
Net Profit:	**$4.45**	Net Profit:	**$5.50**

In this example, you make quite a bit less using the Store Inventory Format, but you avoid potential losses in fees from unsold listings, which is still very important. As mentioned before, listing with store inventory will cost you quite a bit more relative to Fixed Price if your price is approaching the next price break for insertion fees. When you go slightly beyond the next price break your savings will increase tremendously. Let's do an example that shows this.

Example #10

Listing format on eBay: Store Inventory Format

List Price:	$51.00
Shipping and handling charged to customer:	<u>$5.00</u>
Total price charged to customer:	$56.00
Cost of goods from supplier:	$40.00
Cost of postage:	$3.00
Cost of packaging materials:	$0.40

EBay feature fees: none

PayPal rate: 2.9% + $0.30 (based on less than $3,000/month sales volume)

Fees for this example:

If Store Inventory Format:		If Fixed Price format:	
Insertion fee:	$0.10	Insertion fee:	$2.40
Final Value fee:	$4.32	Final Value fee:	$2.09
PayPal fee:	$1.92	PayPal fee:	$1.92
Total fees:	$6.34	Total fees:	$6.41

Profitability for this example:

If Store Inventory Format:		If Fixed Price format:	
Amount charged:	$56.00	Amount charged:	$56.00
Cost of goods:	$40.00	Cost of goods:	$40.00
Total fees:	$6.34	Total fees:	$6.41
Cost of postage:	$3.00	Cost of postage:	$3.00
Cost of packaging:	$0.40	Cost of packaging:	$0.40
Net Profit:	**$6.26**	Net Profit:	**$6.19**

In the previous example the store inventory listing yielded a profit that was $1.05 less than the Fixed Price option. In this example the difference in profit between a store inventory listing and a Fixed Price listing is only $0.07. The only difference between these two examples was that the list price was $2 higher in example #10, bringing it just above the next price break for insertion fees. Why does this make such a big difference? When we raised our price above $49.99, our insertion fee increased by $1.20 for Fixed Price, but remained constant for store inventory. Final Value fees are higher for store inventory than Fixed Price, but we were only looking at a small increase in the price, which results in a pretty insignificant raise in the Final Value fee. This general rule of thumb applies at most of the price breaks ($10, $25, $50, $200) so keep this in mind when deciding which format to use to list your item.

Unpaid Items

Due to the current way in which eBay operates, customers can bid on items, win auctions and never pay for the items they won. Ebay, of course, has policies stating the customer is required to pay for the items they won at auction unless mutually agreed to by both the buyer and the seller, but this policy is not strictly enforced. EBay has a dispute process that allows you to report a non-paying bidder (NPB), at which point the bidder has some time to try and resolve the dispute with you before eBay takes any action. If after a set period of time the dispute is not resolved, eBay will give the buyer an "unpaid item strike", which is essentially a slap on the wrist. If the buyer gets several strikes against them, there is a chance that eBay may suspend them from using the marketplace.

When eBay gives the buyer the strike, they will also issue a Final Value fee credit to the seller, since they were unable to complete the transaction. This is a nice benefit, but it does not rectify the situation. You still lose out on the fees you paid to list the item in the first place (insertion and feature fees) and you cannot get those back. Therefore, unpaid items will have an adverse effect on your profitability. There are ways to minimize unpaid items, such as keeping the lines of communication open with the buyer at all times, sending them numerous friendly reminders to pay after the transaction has been completed. It is also recommended that you write your listing descriptions and policies as clearly as possible, to minimize the number of misunderstandings that can occur between you and the buyer. You can also require immediate payment for all of your Buy It Now items, but this tactic tends to scare some buyers away and would not be my recommendation to implement. In addition, you alienate all other buyers who want to purchase using any method of payment besides PayPal. Since you want to appeal to as many buyers as possible, you should accept multiple methods of payment and not require immediate payment from buyers.

Unpaid items can also result from selling to buyers from other countries. If you are uncomfortable shipping products outside the country for whatever reason, you can state that you only ship within the United States or to countries that you specify. Even if you describe this in your listings, foreign buyers who are not carefully reading your full description will be able to purchase anyway. To avoid this problem there is a setting you can choose in eBay preferences that allows you to block buyers from specific countries. In addition, you can also block buyers with a certain number of negative feedback if you are concerned that they will bid but not pay. Be careful when using this feature; you want to eliminate unpaid items but you don't want to limit your customer base too much.

2

Monitor Unsold Listings To Maximize Profitability

This may be the most important chapter in the book. There are quite a few examples filled with math and numbers, but don't let that scare you off; the ProfitBuilder Software will take care of the calculations for you. It may take you some time to grasp how each individual example works, but the most important thing is that you understand the core concept of this chapter. The most important lesson to learn is to monitor unsold listings carefully to maximize profits for your eBay business and give you the best chance at a bright future as a wealthy eBay seller.

The dramatic effect of unsold listings on profitability happens to be the most overlooked issue by eBay sellers. As your business grows, you will hear more and more people tell you that automation is the way to go and a successful business cannot grow without automation. While there is some truth to this theory it is not all encompassing. The problem with automation is the automated re-listing of your items. Sellers end up with items that aren't selling as well as they originally anticipated, or have taken a recent dive due to a changing trend in the market or increased competition. For many sellers, these listings go round and round, for weeks and months, and ultimately hurt the profitability of the company.

The effect of unsold listings on your overall profitability is going to depend greatly on what kind of profit margins you are working with. In the most competitive industries, sellers work with extremely thin margins and need to watch their unsold listings like a hawk. There have been some big-time sellers in the history of eBay that may have ignored their unsold listings to a certain degree, and ultimately have not achieved the level of profitability they had hoped for when they started the business. You can sell 1,000,000 items in one year and still find yourself yielding a negative net profit when it's all said and done. High volume is pointless without the profitability to go with it, and you may find yourself working 10 times as hard to achieve a tenth of the profits. This book will show you how to ensure your hard work translates to a profitable business.

If you are in other industries with larger profit margins, you may be able to get away with having a number of unsold listings and still remain very profitable. This of course still hurts the profitability of the company, but if you are still producing a solid profit margin when your item sells and are satisfied, you might be alright. The key is to look at how much money the unsold listings are taking away from your bottom line, and see if there is a way to minimize that loss to essentially maximize your profits.

EBay currently has a system in place that allows sellers to receive an insertion fee credit (eBay will give you the insertion fee back that you paid to list your item) if it sells the second time it is listed. This helps keep profitability pretty stable during the first and second attempts at listing, but only gives a credit for the insertion fee. Additional feature fees (Buy It Now, gallery, scheduled listings, etc.) are not refunded the second time and will come right off your profitability if your listing goes through twice. But generally speaking, if most of your items are selling the first or second time through, you are in pretty good shape. If your item has to go through a third time to sell, you may potentially be cutting your profit in half, or even in some cases yielding an overall loss on that item. In other cases, your item may still be very profitable after a number of times listed before selling, but it is important to understand the possible losses that you may incur. Let's take a look at a number of examples that demonstrate how unsold listings can impact profitability.

Each example will show how your profitability diminishes as your item takes longer and longer to sell. See how quickly profits disappear using certain listing formats and features. Remember, even though certain listing features and formats may carry a greater risk of profit loss if the item doesn't sell, these options may create more visibility and attention for your listing, which may improve your chances of selling the item and attaining a strong profit margin. As a seller, you must weigh these factors carefully to decide which features and formats are right for you. These examples are intended to show how your business can be as profitable as possible. Take your time reviewing the examples. If you are confused about a specific number or example, just move on and revisit the example later. The goal is to understand the basic concepts outlined in this chapter so you can make the best decisions about how to operate your business.

Example #11 - Using the same figures from Example #4

Listing format on eBay: Auction

Starting Bid:	$8.00
Buy It Now Price:	$9.00
Shipping and handling charged to customer:	$5.00
Total price charged to customer: (assuming item is purchased at Buy It Now price)	$14.00
Cost of goods from supplier:	$8.00
Cost of postage:	$1.52
Cost of packaging materials:	$0.25

EBay feature fees: none

PayPal rate: 2.9% + $0.30 (based on less than $3,000/month sales volume)

Fees for this example:

EBay insertion fee:	$0.35
EBay Buy It Now fee:	$0.05
EBay Final Value fee:	$0.47
PayPal fee:	$0.71
Total fees:	$1.58

Profitability for this example:

Total amount charged to customer: $14.00

Cost of goods from supplier: $8.00

Total fees: $1.58

Cost of postage: $1.52

Cost of packaging materials: <u>$0.25</u>

Net Profit during 1st listing:	**$2.65**
Net Profit during 2nd listing:	**$2.60**
Net Profit during 3rd listing:	**$1.85**
Net Profit during 4th listing:	**$1.45**
Net Profit during 5th listing:	**$1.05**
Net Profit during 6th listing:	**$0.65**
Net Profit during 7th listing:	**$0.25**
Net Profit during 8th listing:	**$-0.15**
Net Profit during 9th listing:	**$-0.55**
Net Profit during 10th listing:	**$-0.95**

Well, that wasn't so awful. Hopefully it didn't take you more than 7 times through to sell your item, but even at that I would be surprised if you broke even after you factor in your hidden costs, such as providing customer service, and managing and carrying your inventory. Let's break this down so you can see exactly where your profit went each time through.

Listing 1: Same as what we have calculated before.

Listing 2: You received an insertion fee credit from eBay, but you need to subtract feature fees that are not refunded, which in this example is the Buy It Now fee, which costs you an additional $0.05 each time a listing goes through.

Listing 3: Now that your item has gone through twice you will not be receiving any insertion fee credits from eBay. You lost your insertion fee on the first and second listing ($0.35 a piece), and the Buy It Now fee ($0.05 a piece) on each of your first two listings. Therefore, your reductions are as follows:

$0.35
+$0.35
+$0.05
+$0.05
$0.80

Net Profit during 1st Listing:	$2.65
Reduction from unsold listings:	($0.80)
Net Profit during 3rd Listing:	**$1.85**

Listings 4-10: From here on out, you will pay an extra $0.40 (the 0.35 insertion fee and the $0.05 Buy It Now Fee) for each additional time the listing goes through. For listings 4 through 10, profitability has been reduced by $0.40 each step of the way.

Now we will look at the same example again, but this time, add in a gallery picture to see how that changes things.

Example #12 - Using the same figures from Example #11, but adding a gallery picture

Listing format on eBay: Auction

Starting Bid:	$8.00
Buy It Now Price:	$9.00
Shipping and handling charged to customer:	$5.00
Total price charged to customer: (assuming item is purchased at Buy It Now price)	$14.00
Cost of goods from supplier:	$8.00
Cost of postage:	$1.52
Cost of packaging materials:	$0.25

PayPal rate: 2.9% + $0.30 (based on less than $3,000/month sales volume)

Fees for this example:

EBay insertion fee:	$0.35
EBay Buy It Now fee:	$0.05
EBay gallery fee:	$0.35
EBay Final Value fee:	$0.47
PayPal fee:	$0.71
Total fees:	$1.93

Profitability for this example:

Total amount charged to customer: $14.00

Cost of goods from supplier: $8.00

Total fees: $1.93

Cost of postage: $1.52

Cost of packaging materials: $0.25

Net Profit during 1st listing:	**$2.30**
Net Profit during 2nd listing:	**$1.90**
Net Profit during 3rd listing:	**$0.80**
Net Profit during 4th listing:	**$0.05**
Net Profit during 5th listing:	**$-0.70**
Net Profit during 6th listing:	**$-1.45**
Net Profit during 7th listing:	**$-2.20**
Net Profit during 8th listing:	**$-2.95**
Net Profit during 9th listing:	**$-3.70**
Net Profit during 10th listing:	**$-4.45**

Yikes! That gallery picture really killed you if you didn't sell the item the first few times through. Compare your numbers to the results from example #11, which was exactly the same listing except it did not include a gallery picture. In example #11, even if it took 10 listings to sell the item, you only incurred a loss of less than $1.00. In this example, after 10 listings your loss is $4.45. The gallery feature can be a sneaky drain on your profit, but can also be essential in drawing attention to your item. I recommend using this feature when you have a high profit-margin item or predict that the additional attention you will draw to your listing will cause it to sell the first or second time through. If it goes on longer than that, seriously re-consider your listing habits. The reason extra features can drain your profits is because you have to pay for them each time the listing goes through. So, if the item takes 10 listings to sell, you would have paid a total of $3.50 to have the gallery picture with the listing. Again, let's break it down so that we can see exactly where your profit went each time through.

Listing 1: Same as always.

Listing 2: You received an insertion fee credit from eBay, but you need to subtract feature fees that are not refunded, which in this example is the Buy It Now and gallery fee, which costs you an additional $0.05 and $0.35 each time a listing goes through.

Listing 3: Now that your item has gone through twice you will not be receiving any insertion fee credits from eBay. You lost your insertion fee on the first and second listing ($0.35 a piece), the Buy It Now fee ($0.05 a piece), and gallery fee ($0.35 a piece) on each of your first two listings. Therefore, your reductions are as follows:

$0.35
+$0.35
+$0.05
+$0.05
+$0.35
+$0.35
$1.50

Net Profit during 1st Listing:	$2.30
Reduction from unsold listings:	($1.50)
Net Profit during 3rd Listing:	**$0.80**

Listings 4-10: From here on out, you will pay an extra $0.75 (the 0.35 insertion fee, the $0.05 Buy It Now fee and the $0.35 gallery fee) for each additional time the listing goes through. For listings 4 through 10, profitability has been reduced by $0.75 each step of the way. By listing #5, you are already pretty deep in the minus on this item.

Example #13 - Using the same figures from Example #12, but adding the Bold feature to the item

Listing format on eBay: Auction

Starting Bid:	$8.00
Buy It Now Price:	$9.00
Shipping and handling charged to customer:	$5.00
Total price charged to customer: (assuming item is purchased at Buy It Now price)	$14.00
Cost of goods from supplier:	$8.00
Cost of postage:	$1.52
Cost of packaging materials:	$0.25

PayPal rate: 2.9% + $0.30 (based on less than $3,000/month sales volume)

Fees for this example:

EBay insertion fee:	$0.35
EBay Buy It Now fee:	$0.05
EBay gallery fee:	$0.35
EBay bold fee:	$1.00
EBay Final Value fee:	$0.47

PayPal fee:	$0.71
Total fees:	$2.93

Profitability for this example:

Total amount charged to customer:	$14.00
Cost of goods from supplier:	$8.00
Total fees:	$2.93
Cost of postage:	$1.52
Cost of packaging materials:	$0.25

Net Profit during 1st listing:	**$1.30**
Net Profit during 2nd listing:	**$-0.10**
Net Profit during 3rd listing:	**$-2.20**
Net Profit during 4th listing:	**$-3.95**
Net Profit during 5th listing:	**$-5.70**
Net Profit during 6th listing:	**$-7.45**
Net Profit during 7th listing:	**$-9.20**
Net Profit during 8th listing:	**$-10.95**
Net Profit during 9th listing:	**$-12.70**
Net Profit during 10th listing:	**$-14.45**

Compare these numbers to the results from example #12, (exactly the same listing except it did not include the bold listing feature that costs $1.00 per listing). This feature's effect on your profit is even more extreme than the gallery feature since it costs you $1.00 each time the listing goes through. I recommend using this feature when you have a high profit-margin item or predict that the additional attention it will draw to your listing will cause it to sell during the first or second time through. Just like with the gallery picture, you need to watch your listing to see if the bold feature is really improving your bottom line. If it is not generating enough extra attention to increase your conversion rates or your sales price, you need to reconsider whether or not you want to use this listing feature.

Let's see exactly where your profit went.

Listing 1: Same as always.

Listing 2: You received an insertion fee credit from eBay, but you need to subtract feature fees that are not refunded, which in this example is the Buy It Now fee, gallery fee and bold fee which costs you an additional $0.05, $0.35 and $1.00 each time a listing goes through.

Listing 3: Now that your item has gone through twice you will not be receiving any insertion fee credits from eBay. You lost your insertion fee on the first and second listing ($0.35 a piece), and the Buy It Now, gallery and bold fee ($0.05, $0.35 and $1.00 a piece) on each of your first two listings. Therefore, your reductions are as follows:

$0.35
+$0.35
+$0.05
+$0.05
+$0.35
+$0.35
+$1.00
+$1.00
$3.50

Net Profit during 1st listing:	$1.30
Reduction from unsold listings:	($3.50)
Net Profit during 3rd listing:	**$-2.20**

Listings 4-10: From here on out, you will pay an extra $1.75 (the 0.35 insertion fee, the $0.05 Buy It Now fee, the $0.35 gallery fee and the $1.00 bold fee) for each additional time the listing goes through. For listings 4 through 10, profitability has been reduced by $1.75 each step of the way.

I hope it is becoming clear that adding listing upgrades to your auctions increases the risk of profit losses if your item does not sell quickly enough. Take some time experimenting with each listing feature, but make sure you are monitoring the results of your listings. As you continue to experiment, it will become clear which features are improving conversion rates and profits, and which features should ultimately be left behind for the sake of profitability.

Now that we have seen how much our feature fees can impact our profitability, we are going to examine a Fixed Price listing with no additional feature fees, but will still pose some risk to our bottom line.

Example #14 - Higher insertion fees

Listing format on eBay: Fixed Price

Buy It Now Price:	$55.00
Shipping and handling charged to customer:	$5.00
Total price charged to customer:	$60.00
Cost of goods from supplier:	$45.00
Cost of postage:	$3.00
Cost of packaging materials:	$0.40

EBay feature fees: none

PayPal rate: 2.9% + $0.30 (based on less than $3,000/month sales volume)

Fees for this example:

EBay insertion fee:	$2.40
EBay Final Value fee:	$2.21
PayPal fee:	$2.04
Total fees:	$6.65

Profitability for this example:

Total amount charged to customer:	$60.00
Cost of goods from supplier:	$45.00
Total fees:	$6.65
Cost of postage:	$3.00
Cost of packaging materials:	$0.40

Net Profit during 1st listing:	**$4.95**
Net Profit during 2nd listing:	**$4.95**
Net Profit during 3rd listing:	**$0.15**
Net Profit during 4th listing:	**$-2.25**
Net Profit during 5th listing:	**$-4.65**
Net Profit during 6th listing:	**$-7.05**
Net Profit during 7th listing:	**$-9.45**
Net Profit during 8th listing:	**$-11.85**
Net Profit during 9th listing:	**$-14.25**
Net Profit during 10th listing:	**$-16.65**

This listing starts with a pretty nice profit margin, but drops to earning nearly zero profit by the time the third listing runs. This happens because our insertion fees are high due to our Buy It Now price that is above $49.99. Understand that listing more expensive items for sale carries a greater amount of risk. If you plan to take on greater risk, you will want to find items that have a high probability of selling quickly or providing adequate profit margins in relation to the risk you are assuming.

Listing 1: Same as always.

Listing 2: You received an insertion fee credit from eBay, so your profit remains the same since there are no feature fees.

Listing 3: Now that your item has gone through twice, you will not be receiving any insertion fee credits from eBay. You lost your insertion fee on the first and second listing ($2.40 a piece). Therefore, your reductions are as follows:

$2.40
+$2.40
$4.80

Net Profit during 1st listing:	$4.95
Reduction from unsold listings:	($4.80)
Net Profit during 3rd listing:	**$0.15**

Listings 4-10: From here on out, you will pay an extra $2.40 insertion fee for each additional time the listing goes through. For listings 4 through 10 profitability has been reduced by $2.40 each step of the way. This example demonstrates pretty clearly how an item with a pretty decent margin can turn in to an absolute nightmare if it doesn't sell quickly enough.

The following example shows you how using the auction format with the Buy It Now option compares to running a Fixed Price listing. Using the auction with Buy It Now strategy, you are charged a Buy It Now fee for each time your listing runs. At a Buy It Now price above $49.99 the fee is $0.25 per listing. This will have almost as much impact on your profitability as the gallery feature. Experiment with your listing formats to determine if this kind of a strategy provides you with additional benefits over the Fixed Price format. You may find that selling at a slightly lower price using the Fixed Price format is more cost effective than the strategy used in the following example. You may also find that using the auction strategy drives more buyers to your listing and generates a bidding frenzy. Results will vary from item to item, so the key is to experiment!

Example #15 - Higher insertion fees with the auction format

Listing format on eBay: auction

Starting Bid:	$54.00
Buy It Now:	$55.00
Shipping and handling charged to customer:	<u>$5.00</u>
Total price charged to customer: (assuming buyer purchases at the Buy It Now price)	$60.00
Cost of goods from supplier:	$45.00
Cost of postage:	$3.00
Cost of packaging materials:	$0.40

EBay feature fees: none

PayPal rate: 2.9% + $0.30 (based on less than $3,000/month sales volume)

Fees for this example:

EBay insertion fee:	$2.40
EBay Buy It Now fee:	$0.25
EBay Final Value fee:	$2.21
PayPal fee:	<u>$2.04</u>
Total fees:	$6.90

Profitability for this example:

Total amount charged to customer: $60.00

Cost of goods from supplier: $45.00

Total fees: $6.90

Cost of postage: $3.00

Cost of packaging materials: $0.40

Net Profit during 1st listing:	**$4.70**
Net Profit during 2nd listing:	**$4.45**
Net Profit during 3rd listing:	**$-0.60**
Net Profit during 4th listing:	**$-3.25**
Net Profit during 5th listing:	**$-5.90**
Net Profit during 6th listing:	**$-8.55**
Net Profit during 7th listing:	**$-11.20**
Net Profit during 8th listing:	**$-13.85**
Net Profit during 9th listing:	**$-16.50**
Net Profit during 10th listing:	**$-19.15**

Listing 1: Same as always.

Listing 2: You received an insertion fee credit from eBay, but you must subtract your buy it now fee ($0.25) which is not refundable.

Listing 3: Now that your item has gone through twice you will not be receiving any insertion fee credits from eBay. You lost your insertion fee on the first and second listing ($2.40 a piece) and the buy it now fee ($0.25 each). Therefore, your reductions are as follows:

```
 $2.40
+$2.40
+$0.25
+$0.25
 $5.30
```

Net Profit during 1st listing:	$4.70
Reduction from unsold listings:	($5.30)
Net Profit during 3rd listing:	**$-0.60**

Listings 4-10: From here on out, you will pay an extra $2.40 insertion fee and $0.25 Buy It Now fee for each additional time the listing goes through. For listings 4 through 10, profitability has been reduced by $2.65 each step of the way.

Using the Buy It Now feature in conjunction with an auction in this price range has a similar effect on your profitability that the gallery feature did in the previous examples. The combination of the high insertion fee and the Buy It Now fee is a pretty powerful force working against your profitability if the item doesn't sell quickly. Be sure that you have some pretty strong reasons for choosing to run your listing in this manner instead of simply having a Fixed Price listing at $54 or $55.

Example #16 - Even higher insertion fees

Listing format on eBay: Fixed Price

Buy It Now Price:	$320.00
Shipping and handling charged to customer:	$5.00
Total price charged to customer:	$325.00
Cost of goods from supplier:	$280.00
Cost of postage:	$3.00
Cost of packaging materials:	$0.40

PayPal rate: 2.9% + $0.30 (based on less than $3,000/month sales volume)

Fees for this example:

EBay insertion fee:	$3.60
EBay Final Value fee:	$10.16
PayPal fee:	$9.73
Total fees:	$23.49

Profitability for this example:

Total amount charged to customer: $325.00

Cost of goods from supplier: $280.00

Total fees: $23.49

Cost of postage: $3.00

Cost of packaging materials: $0.40

Net Profit during 1st listing:	**$18.11**
Net Profit during 2nd listing:	**$18.11**
Net Profit during 3rd listing:	**$10.91**
Net Profit during 4th listing:	**$7.31**
Net Profit during 5th listing:	**$3.71**
Net Profit during 6th listing:	**$0.11**
Net Profit during 7th listing:	**$-3.49**
Net Profit during 8th listing:	**$-7.09**
Net Profit during 9th listing:	**$-10.69**
Net Profit during 10th listing:	**$-14.29**

Listing 1: Same as always.

Listing 2: You received an insertion fee credit from eBay so your profit remains the same since there are no feature fees.

Listing 3: Now that your item has gone through twice, you will not be receiving any insertion fee credits from eBay. You lost your insertion fee on the first and second listing ($3.60 a piece). Therefore, your reductions are as follows:

$3.60
+$3.60
$7.20

Net Profit during 1st listing:	$18.11
Reduction from unsold listings:	($7.20)
Net Profit during 3rd listing:	**$10.91**

Listings 4-10: From here on out, you will pay an extra $3.60 insertion fee for each additional time the listing goes through. For listings 4 through 10, profitability has been reduced by $3.60 each step of the way.

This example shows that even an item with a great profit margin can end up hurting you badly if it doesn't sell quickly enough. Fortunately, we do have a good amount of leeway with this item. If it sells during the first three times through you are still in pretty good shape and doesn't go too badly into the negative until the sixth listing. If you have an item like this that isn't selling during the first few listings, take a moment to do some marketplace research and determine why your item is not selling. It may be as simple as dropping your price down by $1.00, changing a keyword in your title or adding a listing upgrade like a gallery picture. If you can make a minor adjustment to get your item to sell quickly (even at a lower price), you will save yourself loads of money.

I hope these numbers shock you the way they shocked me when I first realized how much money I could be losing, regardless of my gross sales volume. If you want to succeed on eBay, you need to take your conversion rates (the number of sold listings vs. unsold listings) and feature choices very seriously. If you don't, you may find yourself with a much smaller amount of money in your bank account at the end of the year than you anticipated. On the bright side, if this happened to you last year, you may be able to turn things around. If you are at the gold, platinum or titanium PowerSeller level, you have probably built up a pretty solid customer base. Use these customers to build on your success. Create a newsletter that your customers can subscribe to and offer them incentives to return for another positive shopping experience with your store. Now that you are actually watching your profit margins and ensuring high enough conversion rates, the customers you have already acquired can purchase from you again and this time you can actually produce the kind of profits you had hoped for when you started selling on eBay.

*Additional examples to help you are located in the appendix at the back of the book.

3

ProfitBuilder Software:

The Most Powerful Tool To Maximize Profits And Analyze Risk

As you can see from the preceding chapter, it is extremely crucial to manage your unsold listings and to be aware of the success of your listings at all times. After analyzing the impact of unsold listings and feature fees on my overall profitability, I decided it would be a tremendous help to have a software program that would do all of these calculations for me. I determined what features were essential to create the best software program available relating to risk and profitability and had the ProfitBuilder Software created. ProfitBuilder performs all the calculations we have done in our previous examples for you automatically based on listing options that you specify. ProfitBuilder also helps you analyze the risk of listing a particular item at a particular price on eBay. ProfitBuilder will allow you to specify the following for your listing:

- Listing format (auction, fixed, store inventory)
- Starting bid, reserve and Buy It Now for auctions
- Expected sales price for auctions
- Cost of goods purchased from supplier
- Cost of postage
- Cost of packaging materials
- List price for fixed and store inventory
- Listing features (gallery, scheduled listings, etc.)
- Payment methods

Based on your inputs, ProfitBuilder will calculate the following automatically:

- EBay insertion fees
- EBay feature fees
- EBay final value fees
- PayPal fees (if PayPal is your chosen method of payment)
- ProfitBuilder Risk Ratio
- ProfitBuilder Risk Level
- Net Profit Margin for the first 10 attempts to sell the item
  - Calculates the effect of unsold listings on your profitability, which is one of the most valuable parts of the software

Below is a screenshot of the ProfitBuilder software so you can see an example:

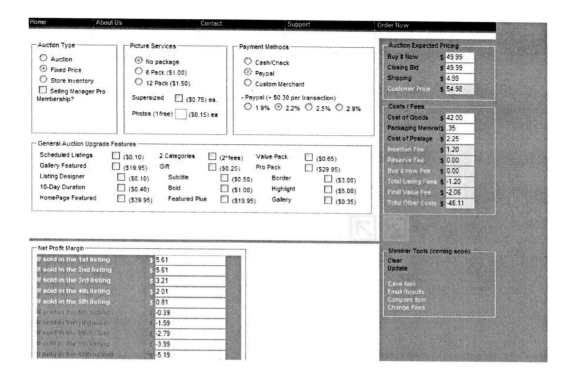

The purpose of ProfitBuilder is two-fold. The first purpose is to assist in product selection and pricing during the product acquisition phase. If you have access to large warehouses full of products that your suppliers offer, how do you know which items will sell? This question will be addressed in Chapter 7: Product Selection. For now, let's just assume that you know the item will sell, but how do you know if it will be profitable? Every time I select a product to sell, I have a detailed understanding of what my profit margin will be on the item if it sells right away and how much risk of loss I am taking on in the event that the item has to be listed a number of times before it finally sells. ProfitBuilder gives you all of this information up front, so you can make an informed decision during product selection and continue to operate a profitable business.

The second purpose of ProfitBuilder is to examine some of your current items that may be problematic. You should run all of your items through ProfitBuilder to stay on top of things, but even if you only check up on listings you are concerned about you will still boost your profitability. As detailed in the examples in chapter 2, ProfitBuilder will show how much money you are losing if your item doesn't sell right away. This information can help you determine what the best course of action is for the item. You may decide the profit margin you are currently seeing is satisfactory and not make any changes to the listing. You may also decide to lower your price to achieve a better conversion rate and a stronger profit, or you may decide that your feature fees are cutting out too much of your margin and ultimately are not worth having in your listing.

Another fantastic feature of the ProfitBuilder software is the risk ratio and risk level analysis. The risk ratio takes the potential profit of selling the item during the first listing, and divides that profit by the listing fees you are charged by eBay each time you run the listing. ProfitBuilder will calculate this ratio for you, and from there calculate the corresponding risk level for you. The risk level tells you on a scale of 1 to 5 how much risk you are taking on by attempting to sell the item using the sales price and listings features you have specified. This is an easy way to alert you to items that may be a little too risky to offer in a Fixed Price or auction format, without a great deal of detailed analysis done on your part.

ProfitBuilder can save you thousands in lost eBay fees and increase your conversion rates. Since you will have a detailed understanding of your risk of listing each item and the profit that can result if sold at various points in time, you will be able to make informed decisions regarding product selection and pricing. You will learn to sell products that provide the greatest profit potential at the lowest risk level. The combination of the ProfitBuilder software and the strategies outlined in this book will be your winning combination to developing a booming business that will make you the next eBay millionaire.

Go to www.profitbuildersoftware.com and sign up for a membership to the ProfitBuilder Software. It is very inexpensive and will save your business thousands of dollars. This will be the best investment you will ever make in your eBay business.

4

Hidden Tips And Tricks To Cut Costs And Boost Your Profitability

The goal of business is to turn a profit. Before you push your business to the limits of a high-volume selling strategy, take a look at your existing business and identify some ways you can cut costs and improve your profitability. Through my experience running my own eBay business, I have developed a number of successful strategies to boost profitability without any increase in sales volume. To start we will look at your costs of doing business. These costs include packaging materials, eBay and PayPal fees, shipping costs, your cost of goods you are purchasing from suppliers and your labor costs and business processes.

Packaging Materials

If you are processing and shipping your own orders, you will need to purchase envelopes, boxes, shipping labels, tape, printing ink and other materials to properly package your products. My business focuses primarily on items that fit into small bubble mailers (envelopes) and we ship several thousand of these items every month. Needless to say, the cost of packaging all of these orders was significant.

We ship a considerable amount of our items via USPS First-Class mail which charges by the ounce. During communications with my processing department, I discovered many of our items weighed only a tenth of an ounce above a weight that would cost quite a bit less to ship (5.1 ounces, for example). The postal service charges 24 cents for each additional ounce to ship via first-class mail. After hearing this I thought to myself, could there be a different brand of envelope that weighs a tenth of an ounce less than the one we use now?

So I poked around the Internet for a while, spoke to a few packaging suppliers, and eventually found what I was looking for. There was a particular brand of bubble mailers that weighed three tenths of an ounce less than the ones we were previously using. To top it off, I was able to negotiate a better price for the bubble mailers with this supplier. My per-unit costs of the mailers were now 12 cents lower than what I was using before. In addition, I was now saving 24 cents per unit on all those items that had previously weighed anywhere from 5.1-5.3 ounces, as I only had to pay the postal service to ship a 5 ounce item instead of 6. All in all for each unit processed I saved 36 cents. Does this sound like saving peanuts to you? Let's take a look at how much this simple move could impact our annual profitability at various sales volumes.

- 10,000 units a year X .36 = $3,600
- 50,000 units a year X .36 = $18,000
- 100,000 units a year X .36 = $36,000

Isn't that shocking? A simple move to a slightly lighter envelope saved my business thousands. If you think selling 100,000 units is impossible, it is actually more attainable than you think (depending on in which industry in which category you are selling). Depending on your volume, this savings could be enough to actually pay your own salary while your business is still growing.

Boxes

Another interesting strategy I have used is the re-use of boxes. Every time you receive a shipment from your supplier, you will be left with a number of empty boxes that can be used. Simply remove the shipping label applied by your supplier and package your customer's order in the same box as long as it is still in good condition. This tactic will likely save you $0.30-$0.60 or more per unit, depending on the size of box you are using.

Free Priority Mail Boxes

In an effort to encourage individuals and small businesses to use USPS Priority Mail instead of other carriers like Fed-Ex and UPS, the postal service now offers free Priority Mail boxes and envelopes. All you have to do is request free materials online or pick them up from your local post office. Without the need to purchase boxes you will save approximately $0.30-$0.60 or more on each Priority Mail shipment you process.

Free Boxes From Businesses

Another potential source of free boxes is from local grocery stores. Businesses such as these usually have a standard way of having their excess boxes picked up and removed from their facilities. In some cases you can call these businesses up and ask them if you could use the boxes they discard on a regular basis. They may allow you to come by and pick them up before they are normally tossed away. If you can set up an arrangement like this and the size of the boxes fit for the kind of packaging material you need for your products, it is yet another way you can avoid paying additional money for boxes to package your products.

EBay Fees

In the previous chapters on profitability we began to think about how eBay fees can impact our bottom line. The first thing you can do to ensure the lowest possible cost is to know your price breaks for insertion fees. Here is a little refresher on what the fees are.

EBay Insertion Fees

Listing Price	Fee
$0.01-$0.99	$0.20
$1.00-$9.99	$0.35
$10.00-$24.99	$0.60
$25.00-$49.99	$1.20
$50.00-$199.99	$2.40
$200.00-$499.99	$3.60
$500.00 and above	$4.80

Be careful when selling directly above a particular price break; you may find you are selling at a higher price but actually making less money.

Example #1 – Fixed Price listing at $50.99

Do not EVER sell an item at a Fixed Price for $50.99! Why? I'll show you.

For the purposes of consistency, we will assume we are charging our buyer $5.00 for shipping, and our costs of packaging and shipping are $0.40 and $3.00 respectively.

Fees for this example:　　　　　　*Fees for this example:*

Selling at Fixed Price of $50.99		Selling at Fixed Price of $49.99	
Insertion fee:	$2.40	Insertion fee:	$1.20
Final Value fee:	$2.09	Final Value fee:	$2.06
PayPal fee:	$1.92	PayPal fee:	$1.89
Total fees:	$6.41	Total fees:	$5.15

Profitability for this example:　　　　　*Profitability for this example:*

Amount charged: $55.99		Amount charged: $54.99	
Cost of goods:	$40.00	Cost of goods:	$40.00
Total fees:	$6.41	Total fees:	$5.15
Cost of postage:	$3.00	Cost of postage:	$3.00
Cost of packaging:	$0.40	Cost of packaging:	$0.40
Net Profit:	**$6.18**	Net Profit:	**$6.44**

If you sold your item at $50.99, you charged your customer $1.00 more than the alternative, and you actually made less money. Plus, by selling at $50.99 with the higher insertion fee, you are taking on more risk of loss if your item does not sell right away. If you sell at $49.99, your profit margin will be $0.26 higher and if you item doesn't sell immediately, you will only lose $1.20 for each additional listing as opposed to $2.40. Using this data, you have a few options how you can list your item.

Option #1 – List Your Item at a Fixed Price of $49.99

This option makes sense because it allows you to offer your customers a lower price, while gaining a larger profit margin than you would at the higher price. If most of the other sellers are selling around $50.99 or higher, your price may give you a little bit of an edge in the market, at least temporarily.

Option #2 – List Your Item as an auction:

Starting bid: $49.99
Buy It Now: $50.99

EBay's fee structure allows you to use this kind of strategy to reduce your fees but still get the selling price you desire. Your insertion fee is based on the starting bid, and will only be $1.20 in this case. To add the Buy It Now at $50.99, you will pay an additional fee of $0.25 per listing. Here is how this compares to selling at the Fixed Price.

Fixed Price of $50.99		Auction at $49.99 w/ $50.99 Buy It Now	
EBay fees		*EBay fees*	
Insertion fee:	$2.40	Insertion fee:	$1.20
		Buy It Now fee:	$0.25
Total insertion fees:	$2.40	Total insertion fees:	$1.45

If you are fairly certain you can get $50.99 for your item, listing an auction with the Buy It Now may be the way to go for this item. However, keep in mind what we learned in chapter 2. Similar in concept to what happens when you add a gallery picture to your listing; if your item goes unsold the extra feature fee can badly hurt your profitability. If you don't think your item will sell right away, you are better off selling at $49.99. This listing method incurs the least amount of risk, and your customers will appreciate the additional savings passed on to them.

Option #3 – List Your Item in Store Inventory (SIF):

In the event your item may take a while to sell, or if you are dead set on getting $50.99 for the item, a store inventory listing may be right for you. With store inventory listings, the insertion fee is always $0.10 per month no matter the listing price (over $25.00). Whether you sell at $49.99 or $50.99, your insertion fee will be the same. Of course, there are drawbacks to store inventory listings, which we previously discussed in chapter 1.

The following is a profitability comparison for all three of the options we are considering. Notice, I have not listed a Fixed Price of $50.99, because that is NOT an option! This example assumes your item sells the first time through, and does not account for the additional risk of unsold listings.

Format	Total eBay fees
Fixed Price at $49.99	$3.26
Auction w/ Buy It Now at $50.99	$3.54
Store Inventory Format at $50.99	$4.42

The least expensive option here is the Fixed Price at $49.99, but you are sacrificing some additional profit you might be able to get using the auction format listing at a higher price. Here is my advice for how you make the decision regarding your listing format. If you are pretty certain your item will sell the very first time listed use the auction with Buy It Now format. This will yield a profit margin of $0.72 greater than selling at a Fixed Price of $49.99. If your expected profit margin on this product is roughly $3.00 or greater and you expect it to sell during the first three times listed, choose the Fixed Price listing at $49.99. I chose a $3.00 minimum profit for this rule because you would have lost $2.40 by the time your third listing sells, which is the last point you could make a profit by selling your item if your original margin was going to be $3.00. If you don't expect a sale during the first three listings and your margin is around $3.00 or $4.00, you absolutely must choose the Store Inventory Format, change the price or listing features, or not sell the item at all. You may also want to think about how many of this particular item you wish to sell each month. If you are content hanging on to the item for a while and only selling every now and again, the Store Inventory Format may make sense to use.

The Second Chance Offer

If you a frequent buyer or seller on eBay you may have heard of the second chance offer. If you have an item up for auction and there are several buyers who bid on the item, you have the ability to offer the losing bidders the opportunity to purchase the item at the maximum bid they entered during the auction (as long as you have multiple units available). This is a great feature to utilize if you have multiple units of your item available for a couple of reasons. First off, this allows you to generate multiple sales from running only one auction. This is a much less risky way to sell multiple items than traditionally listing several for sale, and will likely have a much higher conversion rate. Secondly, the second chance offer gives you to the ability to save some eBay fees. With the second chance offer you do not pay any insertion fee and therefore are only responsible for the final value fee. This can be a big savings, depending of course on the list price. Please refer again to the insertion fee table on pages 12 and 95 to see how much you could save on the item you will be offering.

Create New Listings To Save Insertion Fees

If your item does not sell during the first listing but sells during the second listing, you will receive an insertion fee credit from eBay, provided to you used eBay's re-list feature. This is a great benefit to sellers especially on items with high insertion fees. If your item does not sell during either of the first two listings, you are no longer eligible to receive an insertion fee credit for the item if you continue to re-list it. Instead, after the second listing is unsuccessful you can create a brand new listing for the item instead of re-listing it. By doing this you are creating a brand new item as far as eBay is concerned. This means that you are giving yourself another chance to receive an insertion fee credit. If the item does not sell the third time but does sell during the fourth listing, you will receive an insertion fee credit. The reason this happens is that eBay will treat your listing as a brand new item when you generate the new listing after the second time the item did not sell. Therefore, when it goes through the fourth time, eBay will consider it to only be the second time going through since you generated a brand new listing.

You can use this strategy after each pair of unsold listings, meaning you could generate a new listing for the 3rd, 5th, 7th, and 9th attempts to sell the item. If you do this each time it will give you the option to receive a credit in the event the item sells during the 4th, 6th, 8th or 10th listings. Remember this only gives you the ability to potentially save one insertion fee. If your item takes 10 listings to sell, and your insertion fee for each listing was $2.40, the maximum amount you could save is $2.40; you will not be credited for all of the insertion fees you had paid for the first 9 listings. Take a look at the following example on the next page to see how much you could save by implementing this strategy. We will use an item with a net profit margin of $10.00 during the first listing with an insertion fee of $2.40 as an example.

If no new listing is generated	Using the new listing strategy
Profit during listing 1: $10.00	$10.00
Profit during listing 2: $10.00	$10.00
Profit during listing 3: $5.20	$5.20
Profit during listing 4: $2.80	$5.20
Profit during listing 5: $0.40	$0.40
Profit during listing 6: $-2.00	$0.40
Profit during listing 7: $-4.40	$-4.40
Profit during listing 8: $-6.80	$-4.40
Profit during listing 9: $-9.20	$-9.20
Profit during listing 10:$-11.60	$-9.20

The maximum fees you can save using the strategy for this example would be $2.40, which is the amount you would receive for one insertion fee credit. This example assumed you generated a fresh new listing after each pair of unsold listings, meaning that you created a new listing for the 3rd, 5th, 7th and 9th attempts to list if the item goes that far. You will notice by looking at the chart that you can only save the $2.40 during the 4th, 6th, 8th or 10th listings. This strategy takes a little bit of manual effort on your part but is ultimately worth the time if it ends up saving you the extra insertion fee credit.

PayPal Fees

PayPal fees are tough to get rid of but there are ways to minimize them. The first and most obvious way is to increase your volume. PayPal offers sellers a fee structure based on the total amount of money the seller receives through PayPal.

Monthly Volume	Fee
Less than $3,000	2.9% + $0.30
$3,000-$10,000	2.5% + $0.30
$10,000-$100,000	2.2% + $0.30
$100,000 or more	1.9% + $0.30

There is a possible 1% savings available if you can pump up your volume to big-time levels. For every $1,000,000 of product you sell in a year this 1% savings will add $10,000 to your bottom line. No matter what your annual volume, more than likely there is a way for you to take advantage of PayPal's fee structure by increasing your volume.

Merchant Accounts

Another option for cost savings is to apply for a merchant account through a bank rather than only accepting PayPal. Merchant accounts allow you to accept major credit cards like Visa and MasterCard directly from your customers. There are several advantages to this including rates that can be potentially lower than PayPal. For example, if you are taking in roughly $500,000 a year in sales revenue, you may be able to get a merchant rate of 2.0% + 0.20 per transaction from your bank. Rates will vary from bank to bank, and may be influenced by the bank's opinion of the future potential of your business, so present yourself well when you pay your banker a visit. If you can get that kind of rate from the bank (as opposed to 2.2% + 0.30 from PayPal) you can create tremendous savings for your company. At $500,000 a year the 0.2% savings would add $1,000 to your bottom line, not to mention the savings of $0.10 per transaction. If you did 25,000 transactions during that year through the merchant account, that would create an additional $2,500 in profit for your company. Keep in mind, even if you offer to accept Visa and MasterCard directly from your buyers, a large percentage of your eBay buyers will still use PayPal. It is the preferred method of payment for most eBay buyers. Nevertheless, if you can set up a merchant account at a lower rate than what PayPal is offering, you will still add a significant amount of profit to your bottom line.

Another less tangible benefit to setting up a merchant account is establishing a relationship with your bank. If you plan to be an entrepreneur of any kind (including simply running an eBay business) this will be an important step in launching and growing your entrepreneurial career. The day may come when you are looking for additional financial backing for this company or another business that you start. Obtaining a line of credit from a bank is not always easy to come by. Banks don't care too much about your ideas as they are mainly interested in the numbers you can show them to prove you will have the ability to repay the loan. However, if you have already established a relationship with your bank, all of this will be much easier to accomplish. After utilizing your merchant account for some time, the bank will see your business is legitimate and will appreciate the amount of money your business flows through the merchant account and business banking accounts you have established with them. Once this is the case, your bank will be much more responsive to your business needs and will do what they can to help you accomplish your goals.

There are a few small drawbacks to setting up a merchant account, but nothing that should deter you from doing so. One is that Visa and MasterCard have specific requirements for businesses, such as you must display a phone number for customer service on your website. If you are like many eBay sellers, you may handle all of your customer service inquiries via email and are not set up to have phone support for customers. You will have to add a phone line to take care of this, and have someone to answer the phones, which will add further costs for you to cover. However, you still may be able to fulfill Visa and MasterCard's requirements with only providing minimal phone support for customers and keeping your costs low, so don't let this issue hold you back. The second drawback to the merchant account is the time and effort to implement it. You will need to have several meetings with the bank, and will also need to take some time to have your webmaster integrate the merchant account technically with your website. This is very easy for most web hosting companies to do, but still is something you need to take care of.

Use Your Banking Relationship To Profit on the "Money Float"

Many online retailers use a method of order fulfillment known as "drop-shipping". Using this method retailers create special agreements with distributors to offer any of the distributor's products to consumers without purchasing these products up front. This method comes with its challenges, but allows retailers to offer a wide range of products without carrying humungous amounts of inventory.

For those who are planning to use the drop-shipping model there is an excellent strategy to generate extra money that is often overlooked, which I refer to as the "money float". Here is how it works. Most distributors will sell you their products on credit and give you a grace period before you have to pay. Most often, the distributor gives you, the retailer, 30 days from the time the item is invoiced until payment is due. During this time, you do not pay any interest whatsoever to the distributor. After 30 days, high interest rates begin to accrue.

If you are drop-shipping, you will not order any products from your supplier until the customer pays for it. So, this means you have your money at day 1, and you have 30 days until you have to send the money for the cost of goods to your distributor.

Should you just keep the money in your bank account until it is due or is there something else you can do with this money during the 30 days? Your bank can set up a special account for you that will allow you to earn interest on this money. In contrast to a savings account, this account will be your regular business account so you don't need to transfer any money back and forth, worrying you won't have your money when you need it to pay your distributor.

This type of account is called a "sweep" account. This account is just like a regular business checking account except for one special privilege. The balance remains in your regular account during the day so you can use it for whatever you need. In the middle of the night the funds are transferred to a different bank account that earns interest on your balance. The interest rate varies, but an average rate might be around 4.00%. When you wake up in the morning, your funds will be returned to your regular bank account so you can use them as you please. Basically what this does is allow you to get the benefits of a high-interest savings account without actually pulling any funds out of your regular business checking account.

There are fees associated with a sweep account, so you need to make sure you will have enough money in your account to make it worth your while. Depending on your interest rate, you will likely need more than $10,000 in your bank account consistently to offset the fees. But if your balance will be a much higher amount, say $100,000, you could earn an extra $4,000 a year in interest for doing absolutely nothing except getting the sweep account set up. There may also be a balance minimum required by the bank to open up a sweep account, but once your eBay business picks up this shouldn't be much of a problem.

Another factor that will determine the success of this strategy is the credit terms you have set up with your supplier. If your credit limit is a low amount, like $5,000, even if you are selling $100,000 worth of product each month, you will find yourself paying down your balance every day, and you will not be able to keep enough money in your account to earn enough interest to keep the sweep account going. But if you can negotiate a credit limit of $100,000, and you sell that amount each month, you will be able to keep most of that $100,000 in your sweep account to earn the interest. Obtaining this kind of credit limit is difficult and may take a number of years for you to achieve. Distributors want to give you enough credit to keep your purchase volume growing, but do not want to give you more than they have to. They will ask to look at your financial documents to gather evidence to support your ability to repay the credit line, so you will have to show a high enough level of income and revenue to support the amount of credit you are requesting. As time goes on you will have shown a strong payment history and your distributor will become more comfortable with the idea of increasing your credit line. If possible, ask your distributor if you can get extended terms longer than 30 days. The more time you have to pay, the more you will be able to earn in interest.

Accepting Cashier's Checks and Money Orders

This is something all eBay sellers should do. A considerable amount of eBay buyers are still uncomfortable with online payments. Providing them with the option to send you a certified cashier's check or money order gives your buyers another reason to purchase from you. Additionally, you will not be responsible for paying any PayPal or merchant fees for the transaction. If you accepted a money order for an item that cost $100 you would save $3.20 on the transaction by leaving PayPal and the bank out of it. This will probably occur on only a fraction of your transactions, but is yet another way to boost your profitability.

The downside of accepting money orders is that it will take longer to receive your money. An online payment is instant as soon as your buyer submits it, but money orders can take up to a week or more to arrive via standard mail. In addition, if your buyer is unfamiliar with postal service transit times, they may become impatient and email you inquiring as to why their item has not been shipped yet. This creates additional cost and hassle for you, but is worth the cost savings and additional sales you will bring in by expanding the payment options you offer your customers.

Shipping Costs

Flat-Rate Priority Mail Service

You should always give your buyers the option of upgrading to an expedited shipping service. If you primarily use the postal service, your expedited shipping will most likely be USPS Priority Mail. Fortunately for eBay sellers, the Postal Service has created the flat-rate envelope and flat-rate box for Priority Mail service.

Here is how it works. The flat-rate envelope costs $4.05 to ship anywhere in the country regardless of weight. With regular Priority Mail, it is $4.05 for the first pound and a couple of bucks for each additional pound, depending on what part of the country it is shipping to. You may notice you have items that weigh several pounds, but can still fit into this envelope. If you can get a 3 lb. item into this envelope, you could reduce your shipping costs for that item by $4 or $5, which by itself would be a pretty decent profit margin for an eBay sale in certain industries.

With the flat-rate box, the concept is the same, but the price is different. The box costs $8.10 to ship anywhere in the country regardless of weight. With regular Priority Mail, once you get to 3 lb. or heavier it becomes cheaper to use the flat-rate box. I recall a recent instance in which it would have cost $14.55 to ship a 6 lb. package in a standard box, but the item happened to fit in the flat-rate box so we only paid $8.10. That is a savings of $6.45! If you have been selling on eBay for a while, you will understand how significant a savings that really is. The flat-rate strategy is a great one because it allows you to provide the same fast service to your customers, but adds additional profit to your bottom line.

Free Carrier Mail Pickup

The postal service has also implemented a program called Carrier Pickup, which allows you to schedule a free pickup by a

USPS carrier. Their standard rule is that they will come to any location that ships out at least one Priority or Express Mail package. When I first started using the service, I did not offer Priority Mail service to my customers (a mistake on my part). However, when the Postal Service discovered I would have 50-100 packages for them to pick up daily they didn't seem to mind coming to get them. I now offer Priority Mail as well, and have a carrier come by each day as part of her regular route.

Multiple Shipping Options

You should always give your buyers the option of choosing the way in which they want their item shipped. You want to set your default shipping method as the cheapest one so buyers who are searching on eBay will see the lowest possible total price they can get from purchasing from you, but you will also include shipping upgrades as an option for the customer. Another way to squeeze some extra profit out of each sale is to add in a small premium for shipping upgrades. Let's say for example your item would cost $1.55 to ship via standard mail and $4.05 to ship via Priority Mail, the additional cost to you would be $2.50. If you were charging $3.99 for standard shipping, you could charge $6.50 to cover your additional cost (don't forget you also will have slightly higher PayPal fees resulting from the increase in shipping). On the other hand, you could decide to bump your Priority Mail rate up to $6.99, which would give you an extra $0.50 in profit on the sale. Most likely, a buyer who is in a big hurry to get their item and is willing to pay an additional fee to upgrade their shipping service will also be willing to pay an extra $0.50 for this same service.

Shipping Insurance

There are a number of ways you can use insurance to your
advantage. The first way is to add in a premium for insurance,
in the same way we did for Priority Mail service. The Postal
Service charges $1.35 to insure packages up to $50 in value,
and higher rates for items of greater value. You can offer
optional insurance to your buyers, and instead of charging
$1.35 you can charge $1.95. You can pad this rate because it is
an optional service and you are not forcing the buyers to add it
to their order. Similar in concept to the Priority Mail upgrade, a
buyer who is concerned enough about their package to pay an
additional $1.35 for insurance would likely pay $1.95 for the
same service. When your buyers elect to purchase insurance,
your sale will become $0.60 more profitable. It is acceptable to
charge a premium for insurance because of the time and effort
you have to put in to filing an insurance claim. You generally
will have to make a special trip to the post office and fill out the
appropriate forms. Additionally, you will likely have to refund
your customer immediately, even though the claim has not gone
through the Postal Service yet. The money will come out of
your pocket, while you spend the next several months waiting
for the Postal Service to process the claim and get your money
back to you.

Another way to take advantage of insurance is to self-insure. I
have used this strategy, and it has been proven to be quite
effective. Self-insuring means that your company takes on the
risk of the item being lost or stolen, and will automatically
provide your buyer with a refund or replacement if that
happens. In this scenario, when a buyer elects to purchase your

$1.95 insurance, that entire $1.95 goes straight to your bottom line as long as the item safely reaches its destination. The policy for my business is to self-insure up to $20 when a buyer purchases insurance, but not to self-insure on any item valued above that amount so we don't take on too much risk.

Some might view this strategy as dishonest or unethical because buyers might think they are purchasing insurance through the Postal Service, but it is actually quite the opposite. If you purchase insurance through the Postal Service and your item doesn't show up, getting your money back can be quite a challenge. Investigation as to the whereabouts of your package can take a great deal of time, and there is no guarantee you will ever get your money back under certain circumstances. I have experienced a wait time of over 4 months before I actually received a check from the Postal Service in the mail. If you put a buyer through this misery, you will end up with frustrating emails, a negative feedback and possibly a charge-back from their credit card company, none of which are things you want to deal with. Instead, when we self-insure we offer a refund or a replacement if the item fails to arrive 30 days after shipment. In the end, this is much better service than they might receive from the Postal Service.

Another option is to use a Discount Shipping Insurance provider. These companies serve as middle-men in the insurance business, and will allow you to insure all, or some, of your packages at a fraction of the cost of insuring through USPS. Using one of these companies you can either offer your customers free insurance at no cost to them (and low cost to you) or you can still offer optional insurance and decrease your cost of purchasing insurance by 50-80% over going directly through the Postal Service.

If you use UPS to ship your items they will automatically insure the item up to $100 for free. You can pass this service on to your customers at no cost and advertise that your item includes free insurance, or you can charge for optional insurance if you choose.

Cost of Goods

For information on how to reduce your cost of goods you are purchasing from suppliers, please see chapter 6 on negotiating.

Employee Wages

Think you need to pay high wages to get quality employees? In many businesses this is the method of thinking, but I took a less conventional route. I target high school and college students to be my employees. Instead of posting wanted ads or anything like that, I used my network of friends and family to find my employees. By reaching out to people I already knew, I ended up with a seemingly endless supply of family friends who knew students looking for part-time work. My employees are very intelligent, high achieving students who are fantastic employees. The interesting thing is that I don't pay my employees high wages. So why would these high achievers want to work for me? I have found that students, especially those who want to be top of their class or continue on to an advanced degree, don't have traditional workday hours to dedicate to a job. Furthermore, they don't want to get stuck with an inflexible schedule that makes their life inconvenient. After all, they are still young and want to go out with friends at night and stay out late. This means they don't really want to work at night, and they also don't want to work early in the morning. So when do they work? Because of the nature of an eBay business, most of the work done by my employees can be done at any time. I give my people the flexibility they need, with a small number of weekly work hours and the ability to finish their work at 2:00 in the afternoon or 3:00 in the morning. Of course, there are exceptions for jobs that need to be completed at specific times during the day, but most things can be completed at any time.

Another benefit to hiring these students is they don't need a management team breathing down their neck all the time and making them feel uncomfortable. When I was in high school, I worked at a major retail store that sells office supplies. The job paid pretty well for the kind of job it was, but I was miserable every day working there. I had several managers, one mean old man particularly, who yelled at me pretty much every day. Occasionally it was because I made some kind of mistake, but most of the time I think it was just because he was in a bad mood, and possibly dissatisfied with his life as a manager of a retail store in his late 50's. Needless to say, it wasn't long before I sought out other ways to make money and left that job behind.

My employees are always treated in a friendly manner, and mistakes are treated as learning experiences instead of opportunities for managers to scold them. In addition, there is very little micro-management that takes place within the company. The employees learn how to perform their job in the most effective manner possible, and are trusted to complete their work on their own time. We also encourage employees to ask questions whenever they have any. When employees are comfortable asking questions, their skills increase, mistakes are minimized, and jobs are completed more efficiently. This management method has worked quite well for my company. Our employees learn quickly from their mistakes and strive to improve their efforts because they respect their bosses and appreciate the way they are treated.

Labor Costs and Business Processes

Take a long, hard look at the way you do business and think to yourself, "Can I do this cheaper, faster or more efficiently?" You may find even the simplest processes you and your employees perform have the ability to be improved and can ultimately save you money. Processes such as answering emails, packaging your orders and organizing your inventory likely have room for improvement in your business.

Answering Emails

Do your employees spend hours every day answering emails? If you are not a high-volume seller this may not be too much of an issue for you yet, but some sellers have to deal with several hundred emails every day. For sellers like this, there are email management services out there to help automate the customer service process. While I suppose this does create value for these sellers and cut their customer service costs, I tend to shy away from services such as these. Speaking in generalities, eBay buyers have a propensity to demand more personal attention than your average e-commerce shopper. Therefore, if you implement an email solution that relies solely on automation, your customers are likely to be dissatisfied with your service. As competition to sell on eBay continues to grow, feedback from customers may become what keeps your eBay business head and shoulders above your competition. If you rely too much on canned automated responses to emails you may end up with negative feedback comments complaining of "horrible, impersonal customer service".

So, if we can't rely completely on automated email programs to speed up the customer service process, how can we condense the time spent answering emails and cut our labor costs? A sensible solution is to implement a customer service process that is a combination of manual and automated service. Most emails you receive from buyers will be related to when their item shipped, combined shipping and other general questions. For questions such as these, I suggest developing a frequently asked questions section in your eBay store in case your buyer cares to look. Not all your customers will read these FAQs, but they can help you generate an easy response that you can put right in the email. Simply open up your list of frequently asked questions while you are answering emails, and copy and paste the answer relating to the question asked. This will dramatically reduce your time spent answering emails, while still providing the kind of service your customers demand.

While this will work for many of the questions that are answered, you will still get quite a few questions requiring more personal attention. Questions such as, "Does this movie have French subtitles?", "Do you have multiple copies of this item in stock, and can I get a quantity discount if I buy 10 of them?", or "Is this memory compatible with Sony cameras?" Each will require a human being to answer properly. EBay customers will expect you to provide the friendly, personal service of a small "Mom and Pop" store and the quality and low prices of a giant retailer. This is a tough feat for any eBay seller, but it can be done.

Packaging Your Orders

In the early days of my business many of our processes for packaging orders were very inefficient. The key to spending as little time as possible processing orders is to develop a system that allows your employees to focus on one small, specific task they can do quickly and effectively. Think of an assembly line in a factory. Each worker in the factory is responsible for a tiny portion of assembly that is so repetitive they quickly become an expert on their specific task. While this lack of variety may not be much fun for the employee, it does reduce processing time and increase profits. On the flip side there are ways to make the job more enjoyable for the employees in your processing department. If you are comfortable with the idea try letting your employees listen to music on their headphones or iPod while they are working. This may sound like a distraction, but my employees greatly appreciate this improvement in their work environment, and actually focus better and work more efficiently while listening to music. If your employees are happy, they will work harder for you and automatically improve your business processes.

In the spirit of the assembly line idea, make sure your employees can focus on their task without needing to stop what they are doing to start working on something else. Let me give you an example. As I mentioned before about my own business, most of our items can fit into small bubble mailers for shipping. This allows the employee who is packaging to stay in a stationary position, filling the orders quickly one after the other. However, roughly 10% of our items do not fit into these envelopes and have to be packed in larger boxes. When a larger order comes up, the employee who was processing the orders has to stop what they are doing, go find a box (which has not been assembled yet), assemble the box, then go back and pack the order up. This may not sound like a big deal, but it completely disrupts the flow of work for your order processor.

The solution we found for this problem is to have an employee pre-assemble the boxes needed for the day before order processing begins. We keep the boxes within arms reach of the order processor so when a large order comes up they don't have to leave their position. This sounds like common sense but this simple strategy cut our processing time down by 10%.

In addition to the box issue we also had inefficiencies in the way we pulled items out of inventory to be processed for shipment. In the early days, we only had one person pulling items out to be shipped and then processing the shipments. She would go back into the storage room, pull out as many items as she could carry back to her desk, pack them up and then start the same process all over again. All of the walking back and forth and disruption of her flow of work made her job less efficient and cost the business money. Now that the business has grown, we have employees whose sole purpose is to keep the inventory organized and pull orders to be processed for shipment. All of the orders that will be processed on a specific day will already be waiting, in order, on the processing table so the employees who are packaging can work straight through with no distractions.

Standardize Your Products As Much As Possible

Having a fairly standard product line can help improve efficiency, keep costs low and help ease the business process as a whole. When I say standard product line I am referring to the size, shape and method of storage and shipment for the products. Let's say for example your eBay store focuses on selling electronics. Would you want to sell digital cameras, iPods, cell phones and plasma TVs? I'm sure there are sellers that offer all of these things, but if I were running this business and my company had to process the orders I would likely cut out the plasma TVs. Digital cameras, iPods and cell phones will all likely come in packaging of similar size and shape. Therefore, they can be processed quickly, using the same packaging materials and stored in your office or warehouse in a similar manner. If you had plasma TVs, you would have a variety of new issues to deal with. You would need larger storage space and special packaging materials necessary to ship the individual TVs that might have different dimensions from the rest of the TVs.

Standardizing also allows you to take advantage of quantity discounts on shipping supplies. If you need large quantities of one particular box or envelope your supplier will be willing to give you a better price than if you had to order 20 different-sized boxes. Choosing your product line is a very important part of your business. Just because a product has potential to be bought for a good price and re-sold to turn a profit doesn't necessarily mean it is the right type of product to be sold as part of your business.

Fulfillment Houses

Up to this point, most of the strategies I have described are targeted at the seller who processes orders internally, and stocks inventory at their own location. An efficient alternative to processing your own orders is to turn that process of your business over to a fulfillment house. A fulfillment house is essentially a warehouse that stores inventory for a number of different companies and processes their customer orders.

Here is how it works. A customer goes to your eBay store (or website) and makes a purchase. Through an electronic method of order transmission, usually EDI (Electronic Data Interchange), the order your customer placed is automatically sent over to your fulfillment house. The fulfillment house receives all of the relevant information about the customer and the product to be shipped to the customer. They also receive the customer's preferences for shipping and insurance. From there the fulfillment house will "pick, pack and ship" your order. That means they pick the item off the shelf in the warehouse, pack it up and ship it to your customer. Postage costs are still your responsibility as the seller, but the fulfillment house only passes through the actual cost of shipping, they do not have any markup on the postage. They will charge a handling fee, but this fee is actually a lot less than you might think. The typical handling fee might be somewhere between $0.40-$0.75 per unit. They also charge for storage, but this cost is usually pretty small. If you are working with small margins, this sounds like something that can drastically cut your profitability, but there are undeniable benefits you should be aware of.

First of all, keep in mind this handling fee usually includes the cost of packaging materials, which alone can cost you $0.20-$0.50 or more right there. Don't forget that to process your own orders you will need envelopes, boxes, tape, shipping labels and ink (because you will be printing your own shipping labels). The fulfillment houses have the ability to charge such a low handling fee because of the scale at which they are operating. Since their core business is storing and packaging inventory, they are able to process orders at a much lower cost than you would be able to internally. They get large bulk discounts on packaging materials and in some cases freight discounts as well. Utilizing such an operation allows you to take advantage of the scale of business the fulfillment house has already created, and the benefits of their huge volume are passed on to you.

Second, consider the possibility that your company can grow beyond a level at which you can easily handle at your location and with your current staff. If you outsource your processing efforts to a fulfillment house, you will avoid the costs of growth that create such large risk for emerging businesses. If you tried to handle this growth on your own, you would need to rent out your own warehouse, pay utilities and hire someone to oversee the operation. Not to mention you have additional labor costs for packaging, shipping and receiving.

Another benefit to the fulfillment houses is that you can use a number of locations around the country. As long as they are adequately stocked with inventory, you can set up a situation where the order will be sent to the fulfillment house closest to your customer's shipping destination. This way, you cut down on freight costs (for shipping methods that charge by distance), and you also can dramatically reduce transit time for your shipments. In addition, many fulfillment houses are strategically located at the major hubs for companies such as UPS, FedEx and DHL. Fulfillment houses are often located right off the runway of the airport hubs which allows them to have the absolute minimum cost to ship and receive items.

As with everything else there are challenges to implementing such a strategy. To use a fulfillment house you need to have a very strong system to keep track of your inventory. When you stock inventory out of your own location, you can easily go into your storage room to see what you have in stock and what is running low. With a fulfillment house you don't have that luxury. You will need some kind of system to ensure you have the correct inventory counts at all times, and a system to notify you when you need to replenish certain items in inventory. The other challenge is setting up your electronic method of order transmission. The two options are EDI (Electronic Data Interchange) or a system that generates order reports in the form of a spreadsheet sent to your fulfillment house. There are companies that offer these pre-packaged services, but you will still likely need some help from someone with technical experience to implement your new systems correctly. This also comes at a cost, but the potential growth benefits that can be attained by implementing this kind of strategy far outweigh what you will pay. The trick is making the transition to such a system, while ensuring you provide the same quality service to your customers and keeping your inventory issues under control.

What Type of Business Do You Want To Be?

During the early stages of my business I learned an important lesson. Every business has its core competencies in which it focuses its efforts. I asked myself the question, "What type of business do you want to be in? Do you want to be in the shipping business? Do you want to be in the inventory business, or how about the marketing business?" The answer was clear; my company was in the marketing business, not any of the others. The goal of any eBay business is to market and sell their products to customers, and of course turn a profit. As such, the core of your efforts should be focused around marketing your products not processing orders. You can leave those details to companies whose core competencies are in the inventory and shipping business. If you adopt this way of thinking, you will probably like the idea of outsourcing some of your business processes to other companies. But remember, these strategies are not for everyone. This model works for a number of businesses at different sales volumes, but carries its own costs, risks and challenges.

PART B:

PRODUCT ACQUISITION AND PRICING

5

Understanding Your Role In The Supply Chain:
Finding Products To Sell

In most industries, the product supply chain looks something like this:

Manufacturer

Distributor/Wholesaler

Retailer

Consumer

The manufacturer is the one who produces the product in mass quantities. They have arrangements set up with a number of distributors who purchase mass amounts of product on an on-going basis. The distributor is the one who supplies the product to the retailer. The distributor has to manage millions of dollars worth of inventory they offer to retailers and is responsible for processing the retailer's product orders in a time efficient manner. The retailer purchases directly from the distributor and sells to the consumer. These are businesses like yours that sell on eBay, or on their own website, "mom and pop" stores and major retail chains.

Given this product supply chain, which link in the chain do you think has the highest profit margins? The answer: the manufacturer without a doubt. The manufacturer produces the product internally, and therefore holds all of the cards if their product is in demand and they have few competing forces. Because the manufacturer wants to focus on its core business, which is producing products, it does not attempt to sell directly to retailers or to the public. Instead, in most cases they sell to distributors who act as middlemen between the manufacturer and the retailer.

The distributor purchases from the manufacturers directly, but actually work with pretty low margins. This happens because the distributors focus primarily on volume by selling to major brick-and-mortar and Internet retailers at prices low enough for the retailers to still market their products to consumers.

The retailer, in most cases, purchases directly from the distributor and does not interact with the manufacturer. There are exceptions to this rule depending on the industry and on the retailer's volume, but understand that even major retail chains buy from distributors and not directly from the manufacturer.

If you are just getting started on eBay, do your research first before you jump into a particular industry or product category. If you plan to sell a product for $20, chances are that approximately 50-80% of that cost is eaten up by the manufacturer, with the remaining 20-50% divided between the distributor and the retailer. I made the common mistake of assuming what my profit margins would be before I fully understood the industry I was getting into. Do not assume you can purchase a product for $5 from a distributor and sell it for $20. Generally speaking, this is just not realistic. If the product has the potential to be sold for that high a price, most likely the manufacturer will take more of the profit for themselves by charging the distributors a higher price, which will still be lower than what the distributor charges you. If you research the industry you are getting into, eventually you will get a pretty good idea of what kind of margins you can expect, as it will vary from industry to industry. Also keep in mind that when selling on eBay you will likely have to offer prices lower than retail, which diminishes your margins that much further.

There are different types of distributors and wholesalers, the largest of which are national wholesalers, who are distributors dealing directly with the manufacturers. As I previously described, these distributors have contracts with a small number of manufacturers to distribute their products to large retail chains and sometimes Internet retailers. The popularity of eBay has propelled the small seller's ability to get accounts with large distributors, as they have seen a significant amount of business come from eBay and Internet retailers in recent years. When I first started I hid the fact that I was an eBay seller from my distributors, but now that eBay has evolved I openly share the details of my business with my distributors and they are happy to work with me.

Large distributors have pretty stiff requirements for retailers who purchase from them. The first thing you will need is a federal tax ID number or a resale license. The distributor will ask you to submit this along with your application for an account. Without this number the distributor is not legally permitted to sell to you. In addition, distributors are not interested in dealing with very small companies. Their focus is on sales volume, and will only want to dedicate their resources to your business if they see potential for you to become a large client for them either now or in the future.

Get The Account

If you want to work with a large distributor, your most important objective will be to get the account with them, no matter what the terms. Distributors will look for credit references from other suppliers (if you have any) to show an established track record and credit history of your business. If you don't have any references and the distributor has not heard of you (which they won't have if your business is brand new), it will be difficult to get the distributor to pay attention to you. This does present a challenge, but don't let this stop you from approaching them and getting yourself an account.

When I started my eBay business I was in the same boat. My company was brand new and had no track record or references. Once I knew which distributors I wanted to purchase from, I called them to set up an account but did not have much luck getting a strong response since they had never heard of my company. Nevertheless, I submitted applications and got approved for an account. The initial terms were not ideal, but at least I had an account that gave me the ability to start my business up and start gaining some credibility.

How To Present Yourself To a Large Distributor

When you call a distributor for the first-time, present yourself as either the President of your company or as the "Purchasing Manager." Tell them you are looking at a number of suppliers to see what they can offer you in terms of product pricing and selection. If you have a strong business history, tell them what your company has achieved. If not, give them an idea of the purchase volume you are expecting to do with them and what your sales goals are for the future. You want to think and talk big, but also keep your predictions to realistic and attainable levels. As your relationship with the distributor grows, they will look at what your actual net purchase volume has been compared to what you predicted it would be. If you told them you expected to spend $1,000,000 per month with them, but in reality only spent $10,000 a month, they won't have much reason to trust you the next time you want something from them.

In any event, the most important thing is you get approved for an account. Once you have an account you can show the distributor your business is legitimate which will allow you to negotiate better terms with this particular distributor in the future. In addition, it will give you a reference to use when you approach other distributors in the same or other industries.

Finding a Large Distributor

Locating a large distributor to purchase from can be a challenge when first starting your business. The major distributors do not advertise because they are very well known within their respective industries and do not want to deal with individuals and small start-ups. If you simply do a Google search for "wholesale products" you will find a plethora of less-reputable sources. This is not to say that all of these sources are bad places to get your products from, but they are unlikely to be the large distributors you are seeking out. Instead, do some research and figure out who manufactures the product you want to sell. Usually you can figure this out by searching the Internet or by looking at the retail package that the item comes in. In most cases, the manufacturer of the product will be displayed somewhere on the back of the package. This could be the same as the brand name of the product, but in many cases the product is actually produced by another company. Once you have located the manufacturer, you can call them and ask who distributes their products. Most of the time, they will not have any problem divulging this information.

Liquidators

Another popular way of obtaining wholesale products is to buy from liquidators. These companies obtain their products by purchasing excess stock from manufacturers, retail stores and large retail chains. Excess stock is generated by items that do not sell as quickly as anticipated, or by seasonal items that need to be moved out to make room for new products. Other goods that end up in liquidation can result from customer returns that are no longer in the original packaging. They purchase these products at 10-25% of their standard retail price and then sell to smaller distributors and retail stores. You may also see liquidated products referred to as "closeout" items.

Acquiring liquidated or closeout products can generate high profit margins if you purchase the right products. Liquidation companies all have different policies, but often require the purchase of large quantities of a single product to get the best prices. This can be a decent move for you to make if you can sell the products in a reasonable amount of time, but if you end up with 1000 units of a product you will only be able to sell 5 of every week, you might get yourself into major trouble. Other companies may require that you accept a large lot of items, in which case you do not get to pick and choose, which items you want to sell. In this case, you might as well be rolling the dice at a casino, because you don't know what you are going to get. Even if you turn an outstanding profit on 80% of the items that come in the lot, the other 20% may kill your profitability if you cannot sell them or have to give them away at miniscule prices. Another common issue with liquidation companies is that they may not guarantee that the products you are purchasing are brand new. If you compete in a market that focuses on brand new products, you may want to shy away from liquidators as you might end up with used products you cannot return.

Large Distributors vs. Liquidators

In addition to the differences already pointed out, the key difference between large distributors and liquidators is the supply that is available to be purchased. With a large distributor you typically can get the exact product you want at the quantity you desire any day of the year. You will be able to focus on selling the same products over and over again as additional quantity will be easy for you to come by. Your products will always be brand new and you can count on service from your distributor if something goes wrong. With liquidators, sometimes the supply of a particular product you are purchasing today will be the only supply of that product you will ever be able to get your hands on. This strategy is fine if you are purchasing carefully and producing large profits on these items, but is not without its disadvantages. Any time you consider purchasing a product to sell, you have to spend time researching that product to see if there is enough of a market and margin available to sell that product. If you are buying from liquidators, you may spend more time researching than you would if you were purchasing from a large distributor.

With the liquidation option, you will find yourself researching every time you are about to place an order if you are purchasing items that you have not sold before. With the large distributors, you can consistently sell the same products over and over again, with research done on that product only every once in a while.

There is no magic answer as to which type of supplier is better to purchase from, but one will likely make more sense than the other depending on what type of business you are in. However, keep in mind that many sellers combine the two and sell products from large distributors and from liquidators. This combination of "retail" and "closeout" business is a winning strategy for some eBay sellers. If your focus is generally on brand new retail products but want to offer closeouts as well, you may want to consider setting up a second eBay user ID. This way, your first user ID can guarantee brand new products while your user ID that offers the closeouts can have a completely different set of policies. In contrast to traditional businesses, the ability to create multiple user names on eBay allows you to create separate distinct images for your business. This can be an invaluable asset to your company if you use it to your advantage.

Distributors That Accept Returns

Some suppliers will actually accept returns (some will charge a re-stocking fee and others will not). If you can find a supplier who accepts returns without a re-stocking fee, you may want to consider using their services. I can tell you from personal experience, having a supplier who accepts returns without a re-stocking fee can be a major money saver. Especially when carrying seasonal product (such as items that are only popular at Christmas time), having a supplier who will take back your remaining seasonal product after the demand has passed will be invaluable to your business. Another potential benefit is the ability to return some of your inventory when you are anticipating that you may be a little short on cash for bills coming due in the near future. Your supplier may take a few weeks to credit your account for the returns, but if you plan well this may save you from defaulting on some of your debts and incurring additional interest and penalties.

Keep in mind that returning items without re-stocking fees does not come without its consequences. The largest cost you will likely incur is the cost of shipping the items back to your supplier. This will definitely be covered by you and not the supplier which can drain some of your profits away. The other way that returns can hurt you is by reducing your net purchasing volume with that particular supplier. Many suppliers will offer additional discounts as your volume grows, and potentially even offer rebates to you at the end of the year based on your net purchase volume. If you have pre-determined net purchase volumes you are intending to hit in order to receive a larger discount from your supplier, sending a lot of returns back may hurt you more than it helps your bottom line. While these consequences do exist, they most likely won't hurt your profitability more than having to liquidate your unwanted inventory at low prices, or potentially even being stuck with items that will never sell again.

As I just alluded to, your other option for items you don't plan to sell anymore is to liquidate. If you sell in very competitive markets with high demand, this should be pretty easy. In the most competitive environments, often times a price reduction of $1 or $2 can be enough to move your product out the door. However, if you operate in a niche market with much smaller demand, you may have a much harder time liquidating some of your items even at much lower prices. If this is your situation, hopefully you have a supplier who will take returns so that you don't end up with thousands of dollars worth of inventory that will never sell.

Trade Shows

Another way to find suppliers of the products you want to purchase is by attending trade shows. Trade shows are held in most major cities, and can encompass a wide variety of product categories. Trade shows are an excellent place to make contacts within the top companies that manufacture and distribute the products you are looking for. You will find the major players in the industry, how to buy from them and how to get in touch with them. Each of the major cities in the United States has a convention bureau that you can contact to get information about future trade shows. To gain admission to these shows, you need to show proof you work for a business in the industry. You may need to present them with your sales tax number, bank account in the name of the business, purchase orders and business cards in order to gain entry. Trade shows have these requirements because exhibitors want to present to businesses in the industry and not the general public.

6

Negotiating:

Nothing Is Impossible, Always Ask Questions

If at this point in time you do not have any experience negotiating with suppliers, you probably feel similar to the way I felt before I did my first deals with them. You might think to yourself, "I don't know how to negotiate; I need help from someone with more experience. I can't do this on my own." This can be the most intimidating part of running your eBay business, especially if you are someone who has very little business experience. The truth is that anyone can negotiate; you just need to know what you want, what you might be able to get, and what questions to ask.

What You Want

The subject of what you want seems like a fairly simple issue to address, as you are probably thinking to yourself that all you want is to purchase products as inexpensively as possible to maximize your profits. While this of course is what you want, it is only one piece of the puzzle. Large distributors generally have a wide variety of products related to the categories you operate your business within, and often have different pricing tiers for multiple types of products. Many distributors also have different pricing tiers for items based on the suggested retail price of that item. For example, distributors may get a much better discount on merchandise that has a suggested retail price (SRP) of $100 than goods with a suggested retail price of $12. This means that the distributor may be willing to give you heavier discounts on the $100 item, but not on the $12 item because they don't have much margin to work with. In addition, there may be some products that distributors have thin margins on regardless of their suggested retail price. In other cases manufacturers may regulate the prices at which distributors can sell to retailers, and even the prices at which retailers can offer the product to consumers. In cases such as these, you may run into quite a bit of difficulty if you are attempting to negotiate additional discounts.

What you want to do is pick your battles carefully. Instead of fighting the distributor on your general discount of all products, you will want to figure out which types of products are the most important to your business and fight for those. Will you focus on selling items with a low suggested retail price? Does your distributor offer all types of computer products but you focus on selling hard drives? Whatever your target, know it well and negotiate intelligently for the products that will have the most impact on your bottom line. Using the computer hard drive example, it is possible your computer distributor has the ability to give heavy discounts on hard drives, but not on processors or video cards. If this is the case, you can negotiate a deal in which you will take a smaller discount on the processors and video cards in exchange for a heavier discount than you would normally receive on the hard drives. Since your focus is on the hard drives anyway, this arrangement will improve your overall profitability and will keep the distributor happy. Remember that business is a two-way street. The best arrangement is one that benefits both parties equally. If you can figure out what things are most important to your distributors and balance that with what is most important to your business you shouldn't have a hard time negotiating.

What You Can Get

Understanding what you might be able to get out of your negotiations is very important. To do this you need to research your industry carefully before you enter into any negotiations. Let me explain why. If you simply approach a distributor and ask them what they can do for you, they will come back to you with their standard offer for any new customer. You might scoff at their first offer and say to yourself, "I can't make any money on eBay at those prices; this must be a bad industry to get into. Maybe I shouldn't go into this industry". You might also tell yourself that it must just be this particular distributor that offers bad prices, and what you should do next is find a different distributor. Most likely, this offer is the standard they will offer any new customer and will not better their offer unless you have a long track record in the industry or until after you have proved you will provide the distributor with a consistent stream of high-volume business. If after you have gone to several distributors and they are all offering similar prices, you may have to stick it out for a while at their introductory prices before you can come back to them to renegotiate. Once they consider you a serious client, they may be more willing to negotiate with you.

If you approach one of these distributors without doing the proper research first, you might hurt your credibility by coming across as inexperienced. You don't want to ask your distributor for a 70% discount off of the suggested retail price if the standard margin for retailers is only 15%. It is very important that you understand what the standards are in the industry, because you might find yourself demanding the distributor give you prices far below their cost of purchasing from the manufacturer. Asking for something you can't get doesn't do you any good, and will only hurt your credibility if you make inaccurate assumptions about the industry and the distributor's ability to give you a certain discount.

Ask Questions

Nothing is impossible, always make sure you are asking questions to try and get closer to what you want out of the negotiations. Knowing what questions to ask is half the battle. There are a number of different types of arrangements a distributor can make with you, but most likely they won't offer you any of the benefits unless you ask for them. Instead of always focusing on your product costs, see if you can identify any other areas that can improve your profitability. One example is specific credit terms. Using some of the strategies we discussed in Chapter 4, the way in which you structure your credit terms can greatly impact your profitability. If for example you are using the "money float" strategy, you might want to see if you can get 60-day credit terms instead of the standard 30-day arrangement. In addition, you can always ask your distributor if they will give you any discount for paying early. Some creditors will offer a small percent discount for paying within 10 days and others will make accommodations if you pay cash up front for large orders. Depending on your cash flow situation, some of these arrangements can do great things for your profitability. Some distributors will not consider any of the alternatives I have mentioned, but asking if they can structure your credit in these ways will not hurt you one bit.

You can also ask if your distributor can offer a rebate at the end of the year based on a pre-determined net purchase volume. Some have the ability to do this, and will gladly offer you a rebate to create an incentive for you to grow your sales volume. These rebates are usually for high-volume sellers, but establishing this arrangement when you are small will guarantee the rebate when you finally hit those big sales numbers. If you can negotiate a 1% rebate for example and sell $5 million in one year, you will get a rebate check for $50,000. Benefits like this can be yours, but most likely you will not receive this extra rebate unless you specifically ask for it.

Another thing to ask is if the supplier has specific "break points", meaning levels of sales volume at which the distributor will be able to offer you a larger discount on the goods you are purchasing from them. Some distributors will tell you they don't have these even if they do, because they don't want to guarantee you additional discounts in advance. However, some will reveal their break points and even put in writing the levels at which you will be eligible for additional discounts. This is done for the same reason that rebates are sometimes offered, to encourage an increase in the retailer's purchase volume.

Always make the distributors aware that you have a number of different options and are currently speaking with several of these distributors. Without being demanding you need to make the distributor feel a threat of losing you as a client. If you have accounts with multiple distributors, you can also tell the distributor you are negotiating with that you are considering the idea of spreading your business out amongst a few suppliers. You might tell them you are planning to give half of your business to them and the other half to another supplier. This will hopefully encourage them to go after all your business by offering you volume discounts or the future rebate. They will want to get as much business from you as possible, and therefore will make you aware of whatever ability they have to give you discounts or rebates as your volume grows to certain levels. If you play your cards right, hopefully you will leave the situation with a nice offer from the distributor.

7

Product Selection:
How Do I Know What Will Sell?

When getting started with your eBay business, one of the trickiest issues is deciding what to sell. Deciding on a product line and specific items within that line is not a simple process. Each individual product has its own special market on eBay. Even for a group of similar products, the demand and margins for each of those products may be completely different. In addition, do not select products simply because you know they are in demand. High demand creates competition and competition creates low prices. Even if there are hundreds or thousands of sales of the product you want to offer, the prices may be too low for you to compete and turn a profit. In the event that prices are high enough to create a good enough profit margin for you to compete, the market for the item may be saturated by sellers with too many duplicate listings, causing low conversion rates. Low conversion rates raise the risk that your item will take too long to sell and will cost you money. If this happens, you may choose not to enter the market for this item in spite of its strong demand.

Many new sellers have the tendency to want to break into ultra-competitive industries like electronics or media categories (books, movies, music and video games). For new sellers I have to warn against this move, as you will have a pretty difficult time breaking your way into these categories. Competition for these categories is so intense already, causing profit margins to be very low. If you want to survive in these categories you need to be able to manage a pretty hefty sales volume. The ideal category to get into is something that has strong demand but is not saturated with competition yet. Try and think outside the box. I've met people who sell everything from belly dancing clothing to kitchen sinks.

The product category that is perfect for you may be something hardly anyone else on the planet thinks would be a profitable industry to get into. If you identify the category you want to move into and hear a lot of skepticism from your friends and family, just ignore them. You are the only one who can decide what is right for you. People will always say, "You can't do that", because they don't know how to do it themselves. When I was first getting started, someone I was very close to at the time said to me, "You can't sell on eBay forever", yet here I am years later after taking my business further than anyone believed it could ever go.

Do Your Research

There are a number of research tools available for eBay sellers to determine what is selling in the eBay market. The easiest and cheapest way to research is using eBay marketplace data. This is completely free and is available for any eBay user to access simply by visiting www.eBay.com. The following is a list of steps that you need to take in order to effectively analyze eBay marketplace research.

1) Go to www.eBay.com.

2) Do a search for the item you are looking for in the search box
> e.g. if you are looking for a new copy of "my favorite book", type in "my favorite book" (without quotes)

This will give you all of the results in the market for the book in the eBay marketplace.

3) Once the search results appear, there will be a drop-down box in the top right corner that allows you to search using different criteria such as:
> Time: ending soonest
> Time: newly listed
> Price: lowest first
> Price: highest first
> Distance: nearest first

I have found that the most effective way to sort items is by Price: highest first. This organizes the results for you, so it is easy to see patterns and trends in the market for this particular item. This will show you results in the marketplace for the last 14 days.

4) Using these results, determine if there is enough of a demand for this item for you to sell it. Which criteria you use to determine if this product is right for you is your choice, but I have my own rule of thumb I tend to use. My criteria is that there must be at least 20 listings for this item that sold within the last 14 days, and there must be less than 10 other sellers offering this product. When there are more sellers in the market, I adjust my sales minimums upward accordingly. Keep in mind this model will not fit all businesses. I have a high-volume selling strategy, so I focus on products that will move quickly. Another thing: look at the conversion rate in the marketplace. The conversion rate can be calculated by taking the number of sales in the market and dividing it by the number of total listings. For example, if there were 50 sales in the market out of 100 total listings, the conversion rate would be 50%. Generally speaking, any rate above 35% is pretty decent, and anything above 70% is exceptional. If you are going to accept an item with a dismal conversion rate such as 10%, the item needs to have a very low risk level (see the risk ratio section of this chapter).

5) Once you have determined if there is enough of a market for your product, it is time to figure out if you can sell this item at a high enough price to achieve the kind of profit margin you desire. The ProfitBuilder software can

help you immensely with this process. Pick a price at which you would like to sell the item (see Chapter 8 on pricing for further help with this). Once you have decided on a price, type the price information and shipping and handling charge into ProfitBuilder. You will then need to find out how much this item will cost to purchase from one of your distributors, how much it will cost to ship this item and what your additional costs are for packaging materials. The ProfitBuilder software will also calculate your PayPal or merchant fees for you based on the payment options you specify. At this point, the software will tell you what your profit margin will be if you sell the item during the first time you attempt to list it. In addition, it will calculate your profit margins for the first ten listings in case your item does not sell right away. This feature helps you identify how much risk you are taking on to sell this item, depending on the listing format and features you chose to promote your item.

The ProfitBuilder Risk Ratio

As we discussed in chapter 2 each item you attempt to sell comes with a certain amount of risk because of the threat of unsold listings. When identifying products to sell, it is important to determine the risk of selling that item. We call this the ProfitBuilder risk ratio. This ratio takes the potential profit of selling the item during the first listing, and divides that profit by the listing fees you are charged by eBay for each time you run the listing. For example, if your net profit margin during the first listing of an item is $10 and your listing fees total $1;

you would have a risk ratio of 10. This is a great risk ratio that will provide a low amount of risk for listing that item, the higher the number the better. If your net profit margin is $1 and your listing fees are $1, you would have a risk ratio of 1, which is not a very good ratio and would be a much riskier item to list. The higher your ratio, the lower your risk will be and vice versa.

I have created a tiered system for evaluating this risk that includes five levels. They are as follows:

Risk Level	Risk Ratio	Amount of Risk
Level 1	10 or >	Lowest
Level 2	6.01-10	Low
Level 3	3.01-6	Medium
Level 4	1.01-3	High
Level 5	1 or <	Highest

This tiered system will help you classify your items into different categories of risk, so it is easy to determine whether or not it is worth it to list a particular item for sale in an auction or Fixed Price format. While generally a risk level of 4 or 5 is pretty dangerous, there are factors that can reduce your risk. One thing to keep your eye on is the conversion rate of that particular item. If you are searching for an item you might consider selling and you notice the conversion rate in the marketplace is unusually high, you may consider adding the

item to your product line in spite of its high risk level. Here are
some examples to help you with your decision making:

Risk Example #1

Net Profit Margin during first listing:	$2.75
Total eBay Listing Fees:	$2.75
ProfitBuilder Risk Ratio:	1
ProfitBuilder Risk Level	5
EBay marketplace conversion rate:	90%

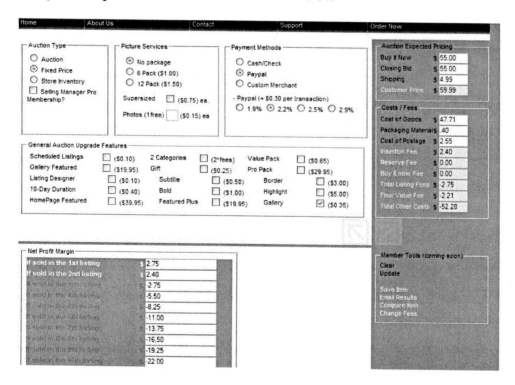

Based on the rules we have instituted, this is a pretty high-risk item and would not be ideal for selling in a fixed or auction style format. As you can see above, if your item does not sell during the first two listings, you will definitely net a negative profit for the sale. If the item ended up taking 10 listings to sell, you would have created a net loss of $22.00. However, the unusually high conversion rate makes this item much more desirable. The risk level is in place so you can evaluate the risk of your item not selling and costing you additional losses in eBay listing fees. But if you are fairly certain the item will sell during the first or second listing, the risk ratio is not something you need to be too concerned about (as long as the conversion rate stays at its current level).

The thing to consider is that a high conversion rate in the marketplace will not likely maintain itself in the long run. With conversion rates that high, you can be almost certain new sellers will enter the market, adding additional listings at lower prices which will drive the overall conversion rate in the marketplace downwards. Conversion rates may also plummet if you researched this item during a point in time that did not yield standard results. For example, conversion rates are much higher during the holiday season because there is increased buying activity for Christmas. In addition, there might be additional demand for the item if it is related to a major event currently taking place. Examples of this could be a major newsworthy event like the September 11th attacks, major sporting events like the Olympics and the Super Bowl, holidays such as Valentine's Day or Halloween and even the premier of a major blockbuster movie. Realize all of these events impact demand, which will affect conversion rates. Once these events pass, conversion rates can drop significantly.

This example points out that an unusually high conversion rate in the marketplace can make a high-risk level item desirable enough to carry for a period of time, but you should always be aware of the risk level of the item in case the conversion rate eventually drops and your item begins to generate a number of unsold listings. Generally you are better off staying away from items with high-risk levels, but high-risk items can be worth a try if there is very strong demand for the item and you are cautious enough to keep a close eye on the demand to make sure the conversion rate stays high and your item can sell quickly enough to remain profitable.

Risk Example #2

Net Profit Margin during first listing: $3.00

Total eBay Listing Fees: $0.35

ProfitBuilder Risk Ratio: 8.57

ProfitBuilder Risk Level   2

EBay marketplace conversion rate: 50%

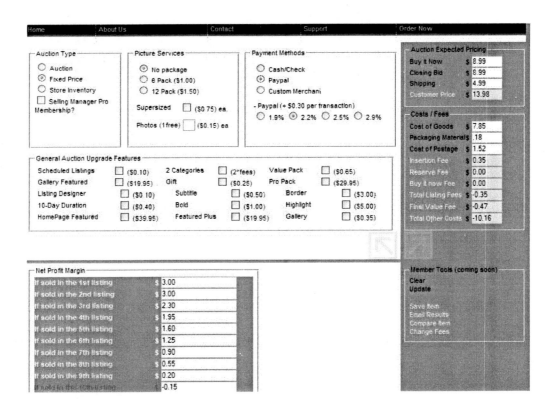

This example shows a pretty low-risk item. If most of your items have risk levels similar to this one, you are in pretty good shape. This is such a good item in terms of risk because your fees are very low in proportion to the amount of profit you would hope to see from the item. As the ProfitBuilder software will show you, you won't hit a negative net profit until the 10th listing through. You also have a pretty strong conversion rate at 50% that suggests you should be able to sell your item during one of the first few listings as long as your item is priced competitively within the marketplace.

Risk Example #3

Net Profit Margin during first listing:	$6.00
Total eBay Listing Fees:	$0.60
ProfitBuilder Risk Ratio:	10
ProfitBuilder Risk Level	1
EBay marketplace conversion rate:	40%

This is pretty much as close to ideal as you can get in terms of a low-risk item. Given the conversion rate you should be able to sell your item pretty quickly, but even if your product does not sell in the first number of listings it is highly unlikely you will ever post a negative profit for this item.

Risk Example #4

Net Profit Margin during first listing:	$10.00
Total eBay Listing Fees:	$2.40
ProfitBuilder Risk Ratio:	4.16
ProfitBuilder Risk Level	3
EBay marketplace conversion rate:	35%

This item would be classified as medium risk. You start with a strong profit margin, but if your item does not sell during the first five listings, you are approaching the possibility of incurring some pretty substantial losses on the eventual sale of this product. This would still be an example of something that might be good to sell, but you will want to make sure the item sells during the first few listings. If the product consistently takes more than four listings to generate a sale, you may want to consider no longer carrying this item or simply moving the item to the Store Inventory Format.

Risk Example #5

Net Profit Margin during first listing:	$3.00
Total eBay Listing Fees:	$2.40
ProfitBuilder Risk Ratio:	1.25
ProfitBuilder Risk Level	4
EBay marketplace conversion rate:	30%

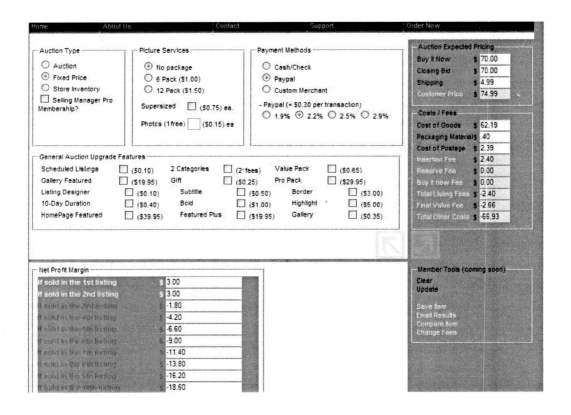

This item is approaching a pretty dangerous risk level and does not have an exceptional conversion rate in the marketplace to boost your chances of selling it quickly. Based on the numbers, my advice would be not to select this item as part of your product line, unless you think it can work for you as a store inventory listing. If you have some kind of edge over your competition like better feedback or more appealing listings, you may be able to make this item work for you. If not, the odds are it will take 3 or more times to sell your item, in which case your net profit margin will end up being a negative. When situations like this come up, remember you are working for profit. If you are unlikely to turn a profit, all you are doing is sending your company backwards and wasting your time and energy.

8

Product Pricing:

Is Being The Price Leader The Way To Go?

Part of the product selection process is to decide how you are going to price your item. In general, buyers come to eBay either for a bargain or to find an item they are unable to find at their local retail store. For the bargain shoppers, low prices are extremely important. Since this will be a large segment of the core customers you will be marketing your products to, the way in which you price your items will be vital to your success as a seller.

When it comes time to price your items, the temptation is to attempt to undercut your competition and have the lowest price on eBay. While this strategy will likely allow you to make a short-term gain in the market, it is very dangerous and I do not recommend it. Let's say the best price on eBay at the current time for the item you are examining is $11.75 and it has a shipping and handling rate of $3.99. The seller who is offering the product at $11.75 is selling at a higher conversion rate than the rest of the competition in the market since their price is the lowest. Since they had such great success with the product at $11.75, you decide you are going to emulate their listing strategy but offer your price at $11.50 with $3.99 shipping so you will be the new price leader in the market.

After you acquire the product and begin selling it at the new low price, you notice you are converting a high percentage of your sales and seem to be snatching some of the sales away from the seller who is still offering the product at $11.75. Soon after, the $11.75 seller (and other sellers in the market), decide to lower their prices to gain a bigger share of sales in the market. Before you know it multiple sellers are offering the item at $11.25 and begin to take a significant piece of market share away from you. On top of this a new seller enters the market attempting the same strategy, pricing their item at $11.00. You decide to fight fire with fire and lower your price to $10.75. You can see where this is going. In a relatively short period of time, your strategy of undercutting the competition has caused the average selling price in the market to drop $1.00. In competitive markets that may have thin profit margins, the loss of $1.00 can be detrimental. If all sellers adopt this kind of a selling strategy, before you know it there will be no profit left to be made on the products they are trying to sell.

The other reason sellers will continue to drop their prices and drive most or all of the profit out of the market is that they may not fully understand their profit margins (unless of course they have read this book carefully). Some sellers think they still have a little bit of margin left to work with and are willing to accept a smaller profit margin if it means they can keep their volume up. Even if they do have some margin left, these sellers may underestimate the risk of unsold listings and the impact it can have on their profitability. These misconceptions may cause some sellers to drop prices to a level below where you are willing to go. If this happens to you, you might want to consider moving on to a different item that will be more profitable and less risky for you to sell.

So instead of undercutting all the other sellers, a better alternative would be to emulate the sellers that have high conversion rates, but without undercutting their prices. Using the $11.75 example we looked at, you could simply offer your product at the exact same price. If all other factors are equal, meaning your product selection, feedback, listing methods and policies are all the same as the other seller, you will likely achieve similar sales. This still may be enough to irritate the other seller enough to lower their prices, but hopefully they will realize that undercutting your price will only hurt them in the long run and will decide to keep their prices constant.

Different Pricing Strategies For Different Situations

How you price your items can also be dependent on how much you paid to purchase the item in the first place. If you got a special one-time deal on a large quantity of a particular product, your pricing strategy may be quite a bit different than if you paid the standard price for the item and were planning to sell it continuously for months or years to come. I'll provide a few examples. Let's say there is an item you would be able to purchase from one of your large distributors for $15 per unit.

Based on your research, the average selling price for this item is around $18 currently. However, you recently found a special one-time deal you could get on 200 units of this product for only $10 per unit. If you take this deal and decide that you only plan to compete in this market for a short period of time to sell off your 200 units and then get out, you may consider undercutting the competition. You could sell at $16 or $17, below the average selling price and blow your competition out of the water in the short run. This can work for you because you need not be concerned about the long-term ramifications of the price war you may be creating in the market. This should allow you to sell your items quickly at high conversion rates, while making the profit you had hoped for when you took the deal in the first place.

Another strategy to use for short-term gains on special liquidations is the auction strategy. If the average selling price in the market is $18 and you are only pay $10 per unit, you should be pretty certain that if you auction off your item you will turn a profit. You can experiment by auctioning off the first unit of the product starting at one penny and see what happens. If you turn a nice profit on the item, you can do this in larger quantities and move your items quickly. Keep in mind that the more auctions you put up at a time, the lower your average selling price will become if you start to saturate the market beyond the level of demand. If you keep experimenting with the number of auctions you put up and are satisfied with the margins you are seeing, continue to add more auctions.

The penny auction strategy has a number of benefits. The first benefit is that you save money on insertion fees. The current fee for listing something below $1.00 is $0.20. Had you listed the item at a Fixed Price of $17, you would have paid $0.60. The second benefit is that you can be almost absolutely certain your item will sell. This eliminates the risk of unsold listings draining your profitability. The third benefit is that penny auctions generate traffic to your listings. If there are 10 sellers currently offering the product around $18, and you are the only seller auctioning it off starting at a penny, you better believe your listing will get more hits than the rest of the sellers. If you have a wide product selection this method can also encourage buyers to check out your other items or your eBay store, and could lead to sales of other products.

Now that you understand some of the benefits of the penny auction, take some time to understand what you are risking. You cannot control bidding activity and can only take your best guess as to what price the auction will end at. Because of this you cannot guarantee you will cover all of your costs by selling the item. When running multiple auctions of the same item over time you will see a wide variety of ending prices. With the example we just looked at you will see some end at $22, $20, $18, $15, $10, $5 and even $0.01. If you auction off an item starting at one penny and the final bid ends at only a penny, the item is not in demand enough to use this listing strategy. Take the one mistake as a warning and move on to a different listing strategy. Even with in-demand items you may experience losses from time to time when using the penny strategy. This is alright as long as all of the auctions collectively turn a profit that you are satisfied with. To find out if this is the case, take a good sample of the auctions that have closed for the item and plug them into ProfitBuilder. The software will tell you what you made or lost on all of the items in total, and will also tell you what your per-unit profit margin is. If the margins are not what you had hoped for, consider moving away from this type of listing strategy.

The strategies I just discussed are ones you would only want to use if you picked up a special deal on an item. If you are purchasing the item at the standard price from a large distributor, you'll likely not want to undercut the competition or run penny auctions. In this case you are very concerned with the long-term conditions in the market and do not want to do anything too drastic to disturb the average selling price for the item. In this case you will probably want to adopt the listing strategy I first mentioned about emulating the successful competition without undercutting their selling price.

Using a "Mixed Bag" of Prices

If you are a high-volume seller with a wide product selection this strategy may be for you. Before we even talk about eBay, let's take a look at large retail businesses and how they price their items. As an example, let's look at mass merchant retail chains that offer low-cost merchandise to consumers in nearly every product category. A few select companies are famous for being the low-price leaders on basically all products. But is this really the case or just a popular misconception? These companies do offer great prices on many products, but if you look closely you will notice not all items at these stores are cheaper than you will find elsewhere. These companies use the "mixed bag" pricing strategy which focuses on advertising very low prices for items in high demand while having higher than average prices on more ordinary items. If you go to one of these stores because they are currently advertising the lowest price around on the summer's hottest new DVD release, you may find yourself picking up other items while you are there such as toothpaste, shampoo or cereal. In many cases, these stores might charge $0.30 more for that tube of toothpaste or bottle of shampoo. Will most consumers realize they are paying $3.49 for the toothpaste as opposed to the $3.19 they would pay at their local grocery store? Often this will go right over the heads of bargain shoppers. This doesn't mean the buyers are getting ripped off by the mass merchants; these retailers are just using a specific strategy that maintains their image as a price leader in the industry while attaining a level of profitability they are satisfied with.

In fact, these retailers often have "loss leaders" to bring people into the store. A loss leader is a popular product the retailer will actually sell below their cost and lose money on. They are willing to accept a loss on this sale, because they are confident if they get the buyer in the store to buy the loss leader, they will also purchase a number of other products at a premium. In addition, the loss leader helps build the image of the price leader for the retailer, and will possibly encourage repeat business from the buyer in the future since they feel they always get great deals from this particular low-cost retailer.

Adapting the "Mixed Bag" Strategy to Your EBay Business

The mixed pricing strategy can be used within your eBay business if you do it carefully. If you have a wide variety of products that you offer your customers you should not have low prices on all of them. Aim to have about 80% of your products priced very competitively with other eBay sellers while the other 20% are sold at a premium above your average profit margin. So which items do you try to sell at low prices and which ones do you target for higher margins? Some people think items that are in high demand are the ones you should sell at a premium. Actually it is the other way around. The most popular items are the ones you want to sell at low-margins because they have the most potential to generate a high sales volume. In addition, offering competitive prices on the most popular items will encourage a large market of buyers to shop from you, ultimately driving more traffic to your other listings and encouraging possible repeat business. For the items that have less demand and will sell less frequently, you can consider using the Store Inventory Format and offering them at higher prices. For these items you don't necessarily need to beat your eBay competitors on price because you are hoping these items will sell as additional purchases a buyer will make while they are purchasing more popular, low-price items from you at the same time.

Using The "Mixed Bag" Pricing Strategy With Complementary Items

Another smart way to take advantage of the mixed bag strategy is to sell complementary products. The goal is to sell the most popular product at a low price, but have other products that are complementary to it that you can sell at a much higher price than what is currently selling on eBay. Making this kind of a sale above the average selling price is what we would refer to as selling at a premium. If you take the iPod example I used earlier, you could sell your iPods at low prices but have iPod accessories in your eBay store that you sell at a premium. There is a decent chance that someone who purchases an iPod may also be interested in accessories, and for convenience sake would rather purchase accessories from you at a premium instead of shopping around for a lower price from another seller. Plus, if you offer combined shipping discounts for multiple purchases, the buyer may save enough money on shipping to make purchasing accessories from you at a premium worth their while. This strategy will work for your business if you identify the right products to be complementary to a more popular item you sell. The reason we normally use the Store Inventory Format for the items you sell at a premium is that they will likely take longer to sell than if you were using a low price strategy with a fixed or auction format. With these items in store inventory you will minimize your risk of loss from potential unsold listings.

Another example of complementary products might be a number of different books by the same author or books that cover similar subjects. A buyer may have a favorite author or might be really interested in books about investing in real estate. If you find the most popular books in either case, you can discount them to be the price leader for that title, but have the other related titles in your eBay store that you sell at a premium. Hopefully buyers will end up shopping from you because of your low price on the popular item, and from there will add additional items to their order that you make a larger margin on. Some of this is guess work and using your intuition, but you can also analyze your past sales to identify good candidates to use this strategy with. You may notice a number of occasions where a buyer bought two particular items together such as an original story and its sequel. When you see these patterns over time you can adjust your pricing strategy and sell the less popular of the two at a premium.

PART C:

RUNNING YOUR EBAY BUSINESS

9

Customer Service:

Be All You Can Be

EBay customers are the most demanding of any e-commerce shopper. They expect friendly personal service, high quality products and bargain prices. In most eBay categories the level of competition to sell an item has evolved to an intense level. As the ability to differentiate your business from other eBay sellers is becoming increasingly difficult, your feedback record on eBay may be one of the only tools you have at your disposal to set yourself apart. If you fail to meet the expectations of your customers in any way, you might find yourself with a less than stellar feedback record that prevents you from achieving your sales goals.

What The Customer Wants

To truly enable yourself to provide the best possible service, it is important to understand what your customers want from their shopping experience. Your customer wants to get a product that is exactly as stated in the auction, they want to be communicated with throughout the entire process and they want to receive their product in the blink of an eye. In fact, most buyers don't just want these things; they actually have come to expect them.

To really get inside the mind of your customer, start by shopping a little bit on eBay as a buyer, and you will find that you will have some great experiences, some mediocre ones and some that are just plain awful.

Scenario #1 – The great experience

You log on to eBay in search of a brand new laptop. You browse around for a while, and come across a seller with a good product description and excellent feedback. Their feedback score is over 20,000 and 99.9% of their customers left them positive feedback. Their description of the laptop states the computer is brand new and describes all of the specs, including pretty much every detail you would like to know about the item. The auction also states you have several options available for shipping. Standard shipping and handling for the item is offered at a reasonable price, and the option to upgrade to an expedited shipping service is available to you at an additional charge. You feel comfortable with this seller and their track record on eBay and decide to purchase. You click the "Buy It Now" button on the auction and commit to buy. As soon as you purchase there is an email in your inbox thanking you for your purchase that provides clear instructions for payment (even though the auction already clearly stated payment instructions). You want your item as soon as possible, so you go ahead and pay instantly through PayPal. After payment has been submitted, there is another email in your inbox thanking you for your payment. This email describes the standard processing time that should be expected before your order is shipped as well as the anticipated transit time once the item has been shipped. At this point, you are very pleased with your purchase and feel everything is going according to plan. The email stated your item would ship out within 1-2 business days. On the next business day you receive another email from the seller stating your item has been shipped. The transit time detailed in the email you received stated you should receive your item within 3-9 business days. On the fourth business day your item arrives at your door. You open the package and everything looks perfect. You start up your laptop, begin to use it and it is exactly as you expected. You log back on to eBay and leave glowing feedback remarks for the seller, hailing them as the "best eBay experience you have ever had!" You felt like you were purchasing from a major retailer, except the price was lower than you would have paid at a retail store and you were very satisfied with the seller's professionalism and friendly service.

Scenario #2 – The mediocre experience

This time, you sign on to eBay in search of a new pair of jeans. You browse through the many options available, and decide upon a seller with a feedback score of 1200, 98% of which is positive. The description of the item states it is brand new, and outlines the measurements of the jeans, which match the size you need. You feel comfortable enough with the seller and go ahead and purchase. Soon after the purchase an email appears in your email box thanking you and requesting payment. You pay for the item, but this time there is no email from the seller stating they have received your payment. A few days pass and you still haven't heard anything more from the seller. You decide to go ahead and email the seller to make sure they have received your payment. The following day they respond and let you know your payment has been received and your item will be processed shortly. The next day you receive an email affirming your item has shipped and will arrive within 3-9 business days. On the tenth business day your item arrives. You open the package and the jeans are exactly as described. You are satisfied with the purchase and received decent service so you decide to leave the seller positive feedback. This service did not come close to matching the exceptional service you received when you bought the laptop, but this purchase was still a satisfying experience.

Scenario #3 – The awful experience

After two pretty good experiences on eBay you decide you want to come back and look for a new CD. You are in a rush and don't have much time to shop around so you look for the lowest price for the CD and click on the listing. The seller has a feedback score of 500, 90% of which is positive. You don't think much about the 10% of buyers who left a negative for this seller, but instead feel comfortable with this seller because you have had other good experiences on eBay, and 90% is still a good amount of satisfied buyers. The listing states the CD is brand new and specifies shipping and handling costs. You are satisfied enough with the listing and decide to purchase. You pay instantly but hear nothing from the seller. After a few days of silence you email the seller to make sure they received the payment for the item. Several days pass and you still don't hear anything back from the seller. You try to be patient but after another week you still haven't heard anything and your item has yet to arrive. You email the seller again to make sure they did receive your payment and will process your order. Another week passes and there is still no communication from the seller and no item has arrived. It is now 3 weeks after the purchase and you are beginning to get concerned. The only email you have received during the whole process was the automated one from eBay congratulating you for winning the auction. On day 36 finally an item shows up on your doorstep. Relieved that the seller didn't run away with your money, you open the package. The CD you ordered that was supposed to be brand new had already been opened. You attempt to be optimistic about the situation, but turn over the disc and see some scratches. Still hoping the CD might work and you might remain somewhat satisfied with the purchase, you try to play the CD. By track 4, the CD is skipping and you are very frustrated. You waited over a month with absolutely no communication from the seller, and after all of that time you were left with a used CD that did not play properly. You attempt to contact the seller, and again hear absolutely nothing back from them. Shopping on eBay has become inconvenient for you and you decide you will just drive down to your local retail store to do your shopping from now on.

These three experiences should give you an idea of what your buyers go through when they are on the other end of the transaction. Keep in mind the buyer I described in these three scenarios is an excellent one. They were very patient and understanding, and gave the seller many opportunities to make things right. Many eBay buyers are like this, but many of them are quite far from being this understanding. A good number of eBay buyers will have unrealistic expectations, regardless of what you state in your auction. You will run into instances where you specify that shipping transit times will vary from 5-14 business days, yet somehow your buyer is upset on the second business day when they haven't yet received their item on the other side of the country. In this example, you even offered a shipping upgrade to 2-3 day service, but the buyer decided not to purchase the upgrade. Nevertheless, you have done absolutely nothing wrong but have an angry buyer on your hands.

Most Buyers Don't Read

Contrary to what you might think most buyers will not read the details of your auction. While I firmly believe every buyer should understand all the terms and details of a transaction they are entering into, I can understand why many buyers will not actually read the auction page before purchasing. If you shop often on eBay you know the shopping process can be a little tedious sometimes. You want to get the best deal so you take your time shopping around and checking out different sellers. While browsing, most of the items and the seller policies seem to be similar, and you may begin making assumptions about the item and seller you are looking at. Because of this and other time constraints, many buyers will purchase or bid on an item without reading the details outlined in the auction. This is one factor that can help explain why some customers have unrealistic expectations and will ultimately be frustrated with their buying experience.

Does this mean you should skimp on your description and not outline every detail of the item and your terms? Whether or not shoppers end up reading, it is your responsibility as a seller to describe your item and policies to the fullest. You will have some buyers who are very thorough and will read everything, and will appreciate the quality of information in your listing and want to purchase from you. This is another way of providing additional service to your customers that can help set you apart from your competition.

Over-Promise And Over-Deliver

At eBay Live, eBay uses the phrase "over-promise and over-deliver" when referring to customer service best practices. They tell you to promise customers the best service possible, quick delivery times and a positive buying experience. These are very important things to promise your customers, but you only want to promise them if you can actually deliver. If you set the bar to a level difficult to consistently achieve, you may constantly disappoint your customers, which is not something you want to do. Instead, make promises that are very attainable, ones you will likely surpass. This way, instead of disappointing your customer, they are pleasantly surprised when they receive their item even faster than they had hoped.

Email Response Time

The amount of time it takes you to respond to emails is critical. For most traditional retail e-commerce operations, all customer service inquiries are responded to immediately with an automated message informing the customer their email will be responded to within 24 to 48 hours. In the world of eBay this timeline is unsatisfactory. If a customer emails you to get more information about a potential purchase, you have a very short timeline to reply if you want them to purchase. The timeline is so short because in most cases there will be a number of other sellers offering the same product at a similar price. Most shoppers are impatient in general, and will likely not wait 24 to 48 hours for you to answer their email. Instead, they will have moved on to another seller in no time. So what's the solution, to hover over your email box all day in case a potential buyer asked a question? Well, we know you can't very well do that. Instead, have a number of different part-time employees who can check emails as frequently as possible. Ideally, shoot for all emails to be answered within 2 hours of when they come in. The quicker you are able to respond to your email questions from potential customers, the larger your conversion rates will be.

Dealing With The Angry Customer

No matter how hard you try to have the most exceptional customer service on eBay, you will always have a number of disgruntled customers. These customers can get upset because something went wrong with their order, but in some cases the customers could have been angry before the purchase even began. Realize that each one of your customers is a real person. They have their own problems, concerns and challenges they face in their daily lives. Sometimes their personal lives affect the way they treat others, and will impact the way they deal with you as a seller.

When I first started my business, I was responsible for every detail of running the business including answering emails. I used to dread this task because sooner or later I was bound to run into a disgruntled customer. Every now and then I would go through email and see a nasty letter from a customer. I have been called a thief, liar, cheat and many other nasty names, in spite of thousands and thousands of glowing positive feedback remarks from customers. Our company prides itself on our feedback record, which is currently 99.9% positive. Even though I knew I was providing stellar service to my customers, every time I ran into one of these emails it put me in a bad mood. After dealing with the angry customer, I would go about the rest of my day but wouldn't be able to stop thinking about the nasty words the customer had written to me.

When you encounter one of these customers, the trick is to keep your composure, and treat them with the same respect you would give to your friendly customers. My customer service manager sometimes tells me stories of unreasonable customers and says, "You know, anyone who treats people this way is not someone I want as a customer." Even if you feel this way (and don't mind losing this person as a current and future customer) you must keep your reputation in mind. One angry customer has the ability to leave negative feedback for you. Even with thousands of positive remarks a few ugly negatives can hurt your reputation. Do everything you can to satisfy your customers, no matter how unreasonable they are. My philosophy is, even if you have to take an occasional loss to give an angry customer a discount or refund, it is worth it in the long run to protect your reputation.

Building Up An Exceptional Feedback Record

If you are first starting out, selling can be a challenge without a strong feedback record. EBay has a wide variety of sellers, from individuals to major companies. Buyers need to feel safe purchasing from you, and this may not be the case if you don't have any feedback yet. To get started, sell some items below your cost and ship them out instantly. Adopting this strategy will likely ensure you will be able to move your items quickly and your customers will be satisfied with the great deal they are getting. Use this method for a while until you have built up a pretty strong feedback record you can be proud of. At that point you can offer products at regular prices and begin to build your business. As I stated earlier don't forget you will still run into a few customers that will be upset with you for one reason or another. Deal with these customers as politely as possible and try to accommodate their needs. A few negatives early on can make it very difficult for you to build up a good reputation and earn the trust of potential customers.

Leaving Feedback For Customers

Many sellers adopt the strategy of only leaving positive feedback after customers have already left positive feedback for them. Others will simply leave positive feedback for any customer who has paid on time for an item they purchased. There is much debate about which is the best way to go, but I think it is a personal choice, and whichever way you decide will work out fine for your business. There is one subject I would like to advise you on though, and that is leaving negative feedback for buyers. As eBay members we are taught to leave feedback for buyers and sellers based on our experiences to create a shopping marketplace that everyone can feel comfortable using while providing warning concerning the "bad apples" out there. However, leaving negative feedback for buyers will hurt you a lot more than it will help you. When buyers receive a negative (even if they are at fault) customers can become angry and want to settle the score with you. Most of them will seek out ways to get back at you, either through negative feedback, angry emails or other annoyances that will consume your resources. Therefore, I tend to shy away from giving negative feedback, and simply move on to more important ways to dedicate the time and resources of my company.

10

The Shipping And Handling Dilemma

One of the most common questions I hear from both customers and emerging sellers I've met when lecturing at eBay Live is, "how much do you charge for shipping and handling"? Customers are very sensitive to this subject because sometimes they feel that even with lower-than-retail prices, the cost of shipping and handling is so significant that it ends up raising the total cost of their item to prices similar to retail and beyond. In addition, eBay sellers are confused as to what they should charge their customers for shipping and handling due to the wide variation of shipping and handling rates that currently exist on eBay. Sellers want to know if they should ship for free, charge customers the actual cost of postage and materials, pad their rates a little bit to earn some extra profit or even charge exorbitant rates far beyond what it would actually cost to ship. Sellers on eBay have implemented every single one of these strategies in many different variations and the correct method is still open for debate.

While there are currently no set rules for how much sellers can charge for shipping and handling, eBay is beginning to notice that the variation in shipping and handling is a problem that needs to be addressed. Earlier this year at eBay Live, Bill Cobb announced that eBay Trust and Safety would begin to go after sellers who charge exorbitant shipping and handling rates. The extent to which eBay plans to crack down on this issue is still unclear at this time, but Cobb mentioned they would start with the sellers that have the most ridiculous rates. An example of what they are going after are sellers who sell items for less than $1 but have shipping and handling rates in the range of $30-$50. Many of these items are not heavy at all; some weigh less than a pound, but sellers are using this strategy to generate more sales and save money. The search results on eBay can be organized by lowest price, which will display the lowest list price first, regardless of what the total price is including the shipping and handling. This means that using this option, the search filter would display an item with a price of $0.01 and a shipping rate of $50 before an item listed at $5 with $2 shipping. The total price on the second listing is more than $43 cheaper than the first listing, but would still show up as being a "higher priced" item as far as the search results are concerned. The other reason sellers would use this strategy is to save money on eBay fees. The lower your listing price, the lower your insertion fee and final value fees will be. Your merchant or PayPal fee will still be the same since it is based on the total amount of money submitted by the customer, but you would save a significant amount of money on your eBay fees.

EBay is going after sellers that use this strategy for a few reasons. The first is fee avoidance. If sellers are able to sell at low prices with high shipping, eBay will lose out on a significant portion of their eBay fees. The second reason, and possibly the more important one, deals with customer satisfaction. EBay wants their customers to have a positive buying experience every time they shop on the site. Customers need to feel they have received quality and value that surpasses what they would receive from a traditional brick and mortar retail store or other e-commerce shopping alternatives. Generally speaking, when a customer is charged $50 for standard shipping of an item that weighs 5 ounces, the customer feels like they are being taken advantage of. This leads to poor feedback for sellers, a negative reflection on eBay's image and the possible loss of eBay users who are fed up with ridiculous shipping rates, even if the total price is still less than what they would pay at their local retail store. EBay realizes they need to fix this problem if they want to continue their growth and complete domination of the world of e-commerce transactions.

It seems pretty clear that you don't want to have your standard shipping rates starting at $30, but how much should you charge? You could choose to charge anything between $3-$10 for shipping, depending on the size and weight of your items. If most of your items are light weight, I would not recommend charging shipping rates on the high end near $10.

There are a number of factors to consider when choosing your shipping and handling rates, the first of which is the fee avoidance issue that we talked about. If you were to sell an item for $8 with a $4 shipping and handling charge as compared to selling at $9 with a $3 shipping charge, you would save a little more than 5 cents on the eBay final value fee. You can see how this would add up for high-volume sellers, especially as you continue to lower prices and raise shipping rates. You do however need to worry about eBay coming after you for exorbitant shipping if your rates get too high. In addition, understand the higher your shipping rates are, the more emails you will receive from customers complaining that your shipping rates are too high. I have received emails from buyers complaining that my rate of $3.99 for shipping was too high, when my rate was lower than nearly all of the other sellers that were offering the same product. As your rates climb, your buyers will become more and more upset with your policies and won't hesitate to tell you how they feel. Ironically at the present time it seems more buyers are interested in purchasing items with low prices and high shipping rates. This of course won't stop them from complaining about the shipping rates, but somehow many buyers still choose to purchase these items instead of going for items with a higher list price and a lower shipping rate.

You might think to yourself that all you have to do is charge a lot for shipping and handling and you will make all of your money that way but this is not exactly the case. As previously mentioned there are a wide variety of shipping rates offered by sellers. Let's say you are shopping for your favorite book which probably weighs less than a pound and probably costs somewhere around $1.50-$3.00 to ship the cheapest method possible. Yet there are sellers that are offering free shipping, some who are charging $3.99 and some who are charging $11.99. How is this possible? Well, you will also notice that the seller who has the free shipping has the highest list price, the seller with $3.99 shipping probably has a list price that is about $4.00 cheaper, and the seller with the exorbitant $11.99 shipping probably has a price that is roughly $12.00 cheaper. The world of Internet shopping is turning to more of a "total price" marketplace where shoppers will focus on the total they have to pay, including shipping and handling, and will most likely go for the lowest total price if all other factors are equal.

The lesson to take away here is that increasing your shipping and handling rate is essentially increasing your price. As of last year eBay began displaying the shipping and handling charges for each seller right next to the list price on the search results page. If a buyer is comparing your item side by side with another seller's identical item, and you are selling at the same price but you have higher shipping, you will likely lose the sale to the other seller. I have illustrated my point below:

Seller	Item	Price	S/H charge
Seller 1:	My favorite book	$9.00	$2.00
Seller 2:	My favorite book	$9.00	$3.00
Seller 3:	My favorite book	$9.00	$5.00

If you were a buyer which one would you choose? Barring any other factors, such as that one seller has outstanding feedback and the rest have pretty mediocre feedback, it seems pretty obvious that most buyers will opt to spend a total of $11, instead of $12 or $14.

Keep It Simple

Shopping on eBay can be a long and tedious process for buyers who are looking for the absolute best deal. To make shopping an enjoyable experience for these customers, you want to keep your policies simple and concise. Some sellers have very complex shipping and handling policies that vary based on the weight and size of the item or even the number of discs included in DVD, CD, video game and computer software programs. The last thing your buyer wants to do after scouring eBay for the perfect deal is to pull out a calculator and figure out how much shipping they have to pay for a 14-disc set based on the policies you have described in your listing. In addition, this kind of strategy feels deceitful to some buyers since they have to dig through your policies and do their own calculations to figure out shipping rates. My recommendation is to keep it simple; have a standard shipping and handling rate that can be applied to any item you offer. An example of this kind of a policy might be $4.99 for the first item and $2.99 for each additional item purchased, assuming the buyer wants the standard shipping service and not expedited service.

The best thing you can do is to be thorough in your research. Before you decide on shipping and handling policies, check out your competitors and see what kind of listings are seeing strong conversion rates in the market. This doesn't mean you have to "copycat" the successful sellers and match their exact shipping and handling policies, but you should use the data in the marketplace as evidence to support your policy decisions. Even more importantly, you should be constantly experimenting with your listings and policies. Selling in the eBay market can be tricky because the lowest total price item doesn't always win. You need the right combination of price, policies, service and product selection to get your items to sell. Continue to experiment and you will discover what works best for you.

11

Start Small, Keep Costs Low And Build From There

When first starting out in business, chances are you won't have a large amount of funds to jump-start your business. While all businesses need some capital for start-up expenses, an eBay business gives you the flexibility to get a little bit crafty and work your way around costs that are necessary for most start-up businesses.

Rent for Office or Warehouse Space:

One major cost you will encounter is that of rent and utilities for any office or warehouse space you may require for your business. When I first started I operated out of a 2-bedroom apartment. There were boxes everywhere and it was a complete mess. Within a few months the business had grown to a point that the space in the apartment wasn't going to cut it anymore, so I moved everything to a family member's home in a neighboring city. From then on, all the inventory was shipped directly there and all orders were processed out of that location.

Operating out of your home can have numerous benefits. You can use the resources already in place to your advantage. No additional rent or utilities to pay, no commute to work and no manager to hire to look after the store at all hours of the day.

While these advantages are essential to a low-cost start-up, do not overlook the drawbacks. Doing business out of your home will dramatically alter your lifestyle. If you are carrying inventory there will be boxes, packing peanuts and other miscellaneous trash all over your home. If you are not careful about organization, your spouse and family may become irritated with you when something related to your business begins to interfere with their personal space or cleanliness. It is also likely you will accumulate a massive amount of large boxes emptied of inventory that will need to be disposed of. Between the pile of boxes out on the street waiting for the garbage man, and the frequent UPS deliveries, your neighbors and homeowners association may develop issues with you as well.

Employees:

Cash is going to be tight when you are first starting your business. You will need money for inventory, office supplies and eBay fees. As you begin to operate the business, you will find yourself doing countless tasks wondering how anyone could possibly have the time to complete all of this work. You will be responsible for answering customer service emails, processing the orders that have been paid for, filing unpaid item disputes for buyers who are overdue on their payment for the item, creating listings for items, deciding what items to sell, and the list goes on. It will be very tempting to hire an employee to ease the burden, but I caution you not to, at least in the beginning. Unless you are dealing with very high margin products that don't cost much to hold in inventory (if you know of such a product, please call me and let's do business together), it will likely be quite a while before your business will generate cash that you can actually put in your pocket.

Quitting Your Day Job

A quick word of advice: don't quit your day job until you feel it is absolutely vital to the success of your eBay business and you are fairly certain you will be able to withdraw the cash you need from the business each month to cover your living expenses. One common misconception about eBay businesses and businesses in general is that a profitable business will always generate cash to pay yourself a salary as the owner and operator of the business. To the contrary, even if your business is doing great, you may need to keep the money invested in the business to pay for inventory, eBay fees and miscellaneous bills. In the early days of my business, I had a very difficult time convincing my family that my business was profitable, since all of my profit was tied up in inventory and I never had any cash to pay my living expenses. So again, be cautious and have some back up cash before you quit your day job.

Fund Your Start-Up By Selling Off Personal Items

The beauty of eBay is that it not only allows you to sell brand new, in-demand products, but personal items you can find hidden in the back of your garage as well. A great strategy to use to get some start-up capital is to go through your house to locate items you currently own but don't use anymore. In addition, you can also check with your friends and relatives to see if they have any "junk" they want to get rid of. You can use all of these products to generate some cash to fund your start-up expenses as well as building your feedback rating up. Your feedback rating is how buyers have rated their experience shopping with you. A strong feedback rating is crucial to the success of any eBay business.

Many eBay sellers started out by selling off personal items they no longer needed to gain experience using eBay and build up their feedback. But unlike most sellers, you can take this a step further and use this strategy to fund the start-up expenses of your new business.

PART D:

INVESTING AND WEALTH BUILDING STRATEGIES

12

The Government Wants
To Help You Be Successful

Contrary to what you might think the government does want your business to succeed. Therefore, they have created many special tax breaks for business owners. The government believes that if a business prospers there will be more people employed and more people paying taxes. If you are successful, you will need employees and there will be more jobs available. When there is an increase in the number of people working, there is a corresponding increase in the amount of taxes people will pay to the government, which is ultimately good for the economy.

The government has all kinds of special write offs and tax incentives you can participate in which are only available to business owners. In order to qualify for these special tax breaks you must establish a legitimate business, be serious about running it with the intent to make a profit and make changes in your operations from time to time if necessary to try to improve its profitability. To be considered legitimate you will have to keep records, have a separate business bank account, take courses that help you to improve your expertise at running your business and possibly hire advisors to help you improve your business operations.

There are many tips and strategies in this book that can help you improve the profitability of your eBay business. The use of the ProfitBuilder Software can help improve your profitability in many ways. It will facilitate your ability to determine which selling format (auction, Fixed Price, or store inventory) will be the most beneficial to provide the greatest margin, will help you understand at what point your items will break even and then lose money so you can minimize unsold listing fees, assist with product pricing, and determine the risk level on items you are considering selling, enabling you to make informed decisions about whether or not selling a particular product will yield a profitable result. Implementing the simple overlooked strategies and suggested business methods I have unveiled to you can increase your profits significantly. With increased profitability you will have more money to spend and more money to invest.

How Operating An EBay Business Can Save You Taxes

Once you have established your eBay business, you can take advantage of the many legal deductions that are only available for business owners. And with the government's blessing you will pay less tax on your eBay profits. You can also convert some of your personal expenses into business expenses, thereby paying less taxes on your other income which will reduce your taxes paid to the government overall. This will enable you to have more money available to get on the road to becoming an eBay millionaire.

There are many tax loopholes, business deductions and tax credits available to the business owner. Some of these expenses you can deduct as a business owner are the same items you now pay for as a non-business owner. For example, if you run your eBay business out of your home, you can deduct part of the expenses that are paid for that home. If your eBay business home office and inventory storage occupies 25% of your home's square footage, you can take 25% of the rent or mortgage interest payment, homeowners insurance, real estate taxes, garbage pickup, gas, electricity, water, homeowner's association dues, Internet access, cable modem, dedicated fax, telephone lines, and more.

You were paying these expenses all along. They came out of your after tax income (the amount of money you had to spend after you paid taxes to the government). By running a legitimate eBay business (even part time), you are now eligible for many legal deductions available only for business owners. The following are a few more examples of expenses you could have as a non-business owner that you could convert to legal deductions as a business owner. All of these legal deductions, and many others, not only lower the tax you have to pay on the profit from your business, but can be used to lower your tax bracket (and the amount you would owe in tax) from your full time job.

If you have children or an elderly parent you support, you can convert part of the money you would give them for allowance or living expenses; just hire them to work for your business. Have them provide a legitimate service for you and what you pay them can be written off as wages (and deducted as an expense from your income). Instead of simply giving them money, and having no tax benefit from doing so, you can give them the money and write it off against your income. As far as the government is concerned, it's as if you never earned that amount of money in the first place! Taking this a step further, you can even pay them wages and then put those wages for them into a retirement account that can grow tax free and start them on the road to becoming a millionaire. We will talk about this government encouraged strategy in more detail later.

Another tax benefit I personally enjoy and use is from traveling. Since you sell on eBay you can always be looking for merchandise to sell. So when you go on vacation you can spend some time looking for some items to purchase and bring home to sell on eBay. Because you are "working" while looking for these items, you can deduct part of the total cost of your trip. By the same token, when you are home and going out to flea markets and garage sales, you can deduct the costs incurred while searching for items to sell including your vehicle costs (which with the high cost of gas really add up), as well as your meals consumed while out searching.

Corporate Filings And Business Structures

When you start up your eBay business you need to make some business decisions. The government has created different types of business structures for businesses. Some are easier to use than others while some provide more asset protection than others. It is important to set up the right kind of business structure to minimize paying taxes and protecting your non-business assets. After all, you want to run an eBay business so you can make more money, accumulate more assets, and minimize your risk of losses. Setting up the wrong structure could increase your risk and defeat the whole purpose of you having an eBay business in the first place.

If you own a business yourself (without a partner) the IRS will consider you a Sole Proprietorship, and you would file a Schedule C for tax purposes. This is a relatively simple tax form and an easy way to be in business, but it puts all of your other assets at risk and increases the amount of tax you pay, not to mention it has the highest risk of a tax audit. If you have a business partner the IRS would consider you a General Partnership. With this type of arrangement you have to split the profits but you have double the risk, as you would take on the risk of both partners.

There are other business structures you can use to run your eBay business which require that you incorporate. They vary in ease of use and amount of taxes charged but they all provide asset protection. The Limited Liability Company (LLC) has become a popular choice for small business owners. An LLC provides asset protection and allows you to choose which tax structure you wish to use with it. You can choose to be taxed as a C Corporation, S Corporation, Sole Proprietorship or Partnership. This type of structure is easier to use than a corporation and has less paperwork but higher taxes.

The corporation structures require more work and forms but have increased tax savings. A corporation is separate and distinct from its owners. It has officers and directors who run the corporation for the benefit of its shareholders (all of these roles could be filled by the business owner). The difference between the S Corporation and the C Corporation is that the money flows through an S Corporation and gets paid out to the shareholders. With the C Corporation there are better available tax deductions and loopholes than with the S Corporation.

To be a legitimate business in the eyes of the government, you need to determine and set up the chosen business structure and your corresponding bank accounts. It is quick and easy to set up the sole proprietorship and partnership. You would need to get a DBA name (doing business as) from your county. Next, you would need to file a notarized form with your County Recorder that specifies the business name you have chosen. If you are a sole proprietorship you would file a Fictitious Business Name form. If you have a partner you would file a form to establish a Partnership. These forms are available from your bank. You need to have your signature notarized on these forms and then file the form to be recorded at your County Recorders Office. Once the form is recorded it will be sent back to you. You will need to take this form to the bank with you so you can open your business bank account.

If you are going to become an LLC or one type of corporation, you will need to file and establish your business as that structure. There are companies you can use that are established to help in filing these business structures for you or you can enlist the assistance of a law firm. These require completing incorporation documents and then having them filed with and approved by the State Corporation Commission. Some of the approved documents need to be published in a local newspaper. Once all of these steps have been completed your business will be considered a legitimate LLC or corporation.

There are some other business processes you will have to put in place to be considered a legitimate business. All legal business structures will need an Employer Identification Number which a lawyer can arrange for you as part of filing for the LLC or Corporation. Another option is to arrange to get the federal identification number from the IRS (available under business at www.irs.gov). You will also need to file for and receive a state sales tax license. For every item you sell on eBay to a person in your state you will need to charge sales tax on the sales price of that item and then report and pay the sales tax to your state periodically. You also may need a business license in your city, county, or state.

This all sounds like a lot of work just to begin selling items on eBay, but believe me it will be well worth it to set all this up to become a legitimate business. Decide which business structure is right for you and set it up right away, then file and receive the necessary documents, licenses and set up your business bank account. Once you have done all of this, you will be able to take advantage of the government's gifts to you as a new business owner.

13

Increase Your Profits Using Business Deductions and Loopholes

It is so easy to increase your business profitability. When you implement the suggestions outlined in this book, use the ProfitBuilder Software to make informed decisions regarding the products you list on eBay, and utilize all the legitimate business deductions and loopholes available to the business owner, there are so many ways to enable additional tax savings. Like I stated before, frequently you can convert expenses you used to pay with personal money (as a non-business owner) into tax-deductible business expenses. How does that affect the amount of tax you have to pay to the government and correspondingly the amount of money you have left to spend and invest?

To pay less tax you have to do any of these three things: You have to decrease your income, increase your tax write offs (deductions) against your income, and/or lower your tax bracket. This can be accomplished as a business owner by finding the common and hidden tax deductions that are available to business owners. When you pay less tax to the government and get to keep more of what you earned, it's as if you had earned more money in the first place.

What are some of the deductions you can take that you might not have thought of? As in the examples given earlier, sometimes you can take deductions for those things you are already spending money on, but as a non-business owner you had to pay for those things with the money left over *after* paying Uncle Sam. What you want to do is make those items deductible business expenses and then you can pay for them with your *before* tax money. Those expenses then add up to lower your income as far as the government is concerned. Then you pay less tax and keep more of what you have earned in the first place. As an employee you receive income, are taxed on it, and then you can spend whatever is left. As an employer you earn money, spend on your tax-deductible business expenses, and then pay tax on what's left.

Start Up Business Deductions

Keep track of all your expenses when you start up your business. These expenses are often overlooked as many of these expenses are paid by you personally before you open your business bank account. Also, don't forget to pay yourself back for anything you had purchased personally and then given to the business. Give a current value to all the items you are transferring over to the business such as office furniture and equipment. Keep track of the totals and then pay yourself back. You can either pay yourself back now or give a promissory note to the business so the amount it owes you is documented as a debt for repayment later.

The following are examples of legitimate deductions and should be written off as business expenses:

Costs of Setting Up Business Structure: Costs of incorporating, lawyer's fees, corporate filing fees, publication costs, DBA county fees.

Cost of Licenses: Business Licenses, State Sales Tax Licenses.

Office Supplies: Paper, pens, packing boxes, packing tape, tape dispensers, paper clips, staples, staplers, blotters, desk organizers, name and date stamps, white out, scissors, markers, rubber bands, post its, glue, tape, packing peanuts, plastic bubbles, postage.

Office and Equipment Costs: Computer and monitor, printer, printer cartridges, printer cables, routers, fax machines and cartridges, copy machines and cartridges, Internet connections, telephones, cell phones, batteries and plugs, headsets, desks, chairs, filing cabinets, tables, wastebaskets, storage shelves, calendars, office décor, postage scale, clock, calculator.

Bookkeeping Set Up: Purchasing Quickbooks or other accounting software, paying for start up accounting services and tax return preparation.

Costs Associated With Selling on eBay: ProfitBuilder Software, Selling Manager, Selling Manager Pro, eBay ProStores (an off eBay website), Accounting Assistant, eBay Store subscription, digital camera.

Costs of Inventory: Cost of anything you have purchased to sell including what it cost to have the products shipped to you. If you are selling some of your own items, give them a value, and then pay yourself that value for the sale of those items to your business. Also include anything you have to purchase in order to increase the value of an item such as cleaning supplies, batteries, new cords, or replacement parts.

Learning and Educational Expenses

The first thing you should put on your list of deductible items is this book, eBay *Millionaire or Bust*. It has been a very important learning tool and is absolutely deductible. Same goes for the purchase of the *ProfitBuilder Software*. Also included in this category would be anything that helps you learn more about eBay, running a business, bookkeeping, record keeping, how to take better photos for your eBay listings, how to write a business plan, how to be an entrepreneur, how to save on taxes, how to invest your earnings to become a millionaire, all seminars, workshops, online courses, educational products, money you spend on your financial and accounting advisors, even all your expenses for your trip to the next eBay Live.

Daily Business Expenses

Don't forget any of the costs related to the daily operation of your business. You can deduct your PayPal and eBay fees, the cost of purchasing your goods, bad debts (sales that were never paid for), advertising fees such as eBay keywords, pay per click advertising, newspaper and magazine advertising, and the cost of designing and operating a website. You can also deduct contributions to charities, cost of publicity, attorney fees for any business purpose, employee expenses, checking account bank charges, commissions paid to salespeople, employees, cost of attending conventions, dues to belong to professional organizations, entertainment expenses, freight charges, health insurance premiums, business insurance premiums, interest expenses, damaged inventory, newspapers, telephone and cell phone charges, office stationery, social security and other taxes paid for employees, subscriptions to trade, business and professional organizations.

Also don't forget you can deduct the costs of driving to the post office, picking up supplies and looking around town for items to buy and sell. That would include your automobile expenses and the costs of meals while you were out looking for products. If you went away for the weekend to a neighboring town to look through antique stores, art stores, flea markets and more you can deduct the costs of making that trip. Any seminar you attend in or out of town you could also deduct, including your transportation to get there.

Auto Expenses

There are two different ways of calculating the deductible costs of using your auto for business. You can either add up all the costs for the year for gas and oil, tires, repairs, insurance fees, loan or lease payments, license fees, the cost to store your vehicle and depreciation, and divide it by the percentage of business miles driven. Otherwise, you can take a per mile charge for each mile that you have driven your vehicle for business related purposes. For 2006 that per mile deduction is 44.5 cents per mile driven. You need to keep good records of how many miles you have driven. An easy way to do that is to keep a spiral notebook in your glove compartment and make note of business miles driven each day.

There are some special deductions that apply to driving different types of vehicles and based on the way you pay for your vehicle. If you lease a vehicle you could end up with higher tax write offs than if you depreciate your vehicle. Neither of these write offs are available to non-business owners of vehicles. In 2005 there was a SUV tax loophole. If you purchased a new or used vehicle that was more than 6000 lbs, you could deduct it up to $25,000 the year it was put in service. In this case, the vehicle was treated as if it was a piece of capital equipment rather than as a vehicle. This was a great write off for anyone who needed a large vehicle. When running an eBay business it could be very beneficial to have a large vehicle that could accommodate large purchases. There was also a special deduction for hybrid vehicles. Tax write offs are constantly being amended so be sure to check with an accountant for the current special write offs that might apply to your vehicles.

Meal and Travel Expenses

You can deduct meal and travel expenses when you are doing business related activities. Whenever you are out for a meal and you discuss your business you can deduct 50% of that meal. Keep your receipts and be sure to keep notes of who you were with and what you discussed. You can also deduct 50% of the meals you eat while looking for merchandise to sell on eBay whether in town or out of town. Just keep the receipts. When traveling within the United States you can deduct the travel expenses incurred for your trip if you are working for part of the trip. That could include looking for merchandise to purchase for resale on eBay, checking eBay listings and answering emails at an Internet café or from the hotel business center or hotel room if it had Internet access. You can deduct all or part of your hotel, transportation, car rental, train, and gas expenses. While traveling abroad you can deduct a percentage of the overall costs of the trip depending upon the number of days you work compared to the whole trip. Keep a list of stores you visited looking for merchandise, time spent at Internet cafes, and of course, keep your receipts.

Also there are special travel tax deductions that apply if you become an LLC or Corporation. One of the requirements for corporations is to have an Annual Meeting; for the LLC it is optional. You are allowed to take a deduction for the expenses incurred to have that meeting, so you can be on vacation and hold the annual meeting and part of the cost of the vacation will be deductible.

Medical Expenses

You have more options to write off medical expenses as an employer than as an employee. When you are self-employed (schedule C) you are able to deduct your medical insurance coverage. You can now deduct 100% of what you spend for medical insurance. Both the S corporations and C corporations can provide healthcare coverage for their employees. With a C Corporation you can have medical insurance or design a medical reimbursement plan. It may also be easier to get medical coverage approved when you are a corporation rather than just a sole proprietorship.

Special Loopholes For Homeowners

There are special loopholes for the home based business owner. In addition to being able to take off a percentage of the mortgage payment and utilities for the business use of the home, there are a few other things that only apply for homeowners. One loophole is that you can deduct what you spend to fix up or remodel your home office or make changes to your home to accommodate more storage, repainting, putting up shelves, or converting an old bedroom into an office or workroom. You can also deduct the portion of your home where you have inventory stored in addition to what you can deduct for your home office. In addition, you can depreciate part of the value of your home attributable to the percentage of business use of your home. All of these would create further tax deductions you can use to reduce the amount of tax you would have to pay Uncle Sam. Whatever amount of tax you can deduct and not have to give to the government is the equivalent of making that much more profit from your business.

There are other overlooked benefits of having a home based business when you own your home. Your home is probably your largest appreciating asset. Part of the money that is paying for the upkeep of your home is deductible when you have a home office. The money you are paying for your home business office is contributing to a potential increase in your net worth. Real estate ownership is traditionally one of the best investments you can make as home values generally appreciate. The total value of the home appreciates rather than the amount you have invested in the home. So as an example, if the value of your home is $250,000 and it appreciates by 10% in one year, the home goes up in value by $25,000 that year. And maybe you had only initially invested $10,000 in that home. So in the year where your home went up $25,000 that is 250% of your original investment. The amount that you pay for the mortgage and utilities that you can deduct as a business expense not only reduces the amount of tax you owe the government but contributes to the increase in your net worth. This is in contrast to paying to rent or lease office space. When you rent or lease office space you can deduct those costs but do not get the additional benefit of appreciation. The only way to get appreciation on what you pay for office space outside the home is to own the building that houses your office space.

A possible strategy to implement as your business grows would be to trade up to a larger home rather than pay to rent or lease office space somewhere. Your eBay business can create the ability for you to write off larger amounts of money as the expenses for your home office increase. If you buy a more expensive home, you will have higher mortgage and utility costs. You can continue to deduct part of these higher amounts as long as you continue to run your eBay business. Real estate appreciation is based on the value of the home not the amount of investment in the home. So if you have a home, for example, that is worth $400,000 and you make the same 10% appreciation in one year, your home will increase by $40,000. That is $40,000 appreciation versus the previously mentioned $25,000 appreciation for one year's time only. Think about how that would add up over the years. You will have higher payments on a $400,000 home versus a $250,000 home, but your eBay business and tax write offs will help subsidize the larger appreciation and subsequent potential increases to your net worth.

Also keep in mind that the government allows part of the increased appreciation of your home to be excluded from taxation when you sell your home. Single homeowners can exclude the first $250,000 of gain on their home from taxation and married homeowners can exclude the first $500,000 of gain on their home from taxation. There may be some recapture of depreciation taken for your home office deducted from these amounts, but this increases your ability to build your net worth. And when you run an eBay business out of your home, you are able to deduct part of the expenses of paying for your home ownership as your asset appreciates and your net worth builds.

14

Become An EBay Millionaire

Anyone with an eBay business can become a millionaire. Follow my suggestions and tips to increase your profits, reduce your taxes, keep more of what you make, and have it grow so you can become a millionaire. Regardless of how much money you make selling on eBay, you can become a millionaire. Having an eBay business changes everything for you. Because you have a legitimate business, you now qualify for special tax treatment, allowing you to pay for things out of before tax dollars and lower what you pay the government. That tax savings translates to more money in your pocket, and part of that money can work for you to make you a millionaire.

The government wants you to be successful. That's why they have created special programs for you as a business owner and investor. They have created many options for the business owner to invest for retirement. There are IRAs, 401Ks, Simple IRAS and various types of Profit Sharing Plans. Generally, a business owner can set aside as much as 25% of their net income up to $44,000 per year for Profit Sharing Plans, up to $15,000 per year into 401K's, up to $10,000 per year into Simple IRAS and up to $4000 per year into IRAS. Once Americans turn 50 years old, they can contribute more than these amounts to catch up for their retirement since they don't have as long to save. Amounts contributed to these retirement savings plans by all Americans grow without taxation.

Follow this strategy to turn your eBay business into a profit-producing machine. Take part of the amount you make from your eBay business to buy a home (to be able to take advantage of home office deductions and the subsequent subsidy to your home appreciation), and then contribute to some type of retirement account. You would be surprised how much money you can accumulate! If you contribute to a Roth IRA or Roth 401K in these following examples the money you accumulate in them will be tax-free forever!

Investment Example #1

If you can invest $4,000 annually and earn an average 10% compounded return you would accumulate $1,000,000 in approximately 33 years.

If you could earn 15% compounded return on a $4,000 yearly investment you would accumulate $1,000,000 in approximately 25 years.

Investment Example #2

If you and your spouse each contributed the $4,000 annually with an average 10% compounded return you would accumulate $1,000,000 in approximately 26 years.

If you and your spouse each contributed the $4,000 annually with an average 15% compounded return you would accumulate $1,000,000 in approximately 20 years.

Investment Example #3

If you contribute larger amounts you would get to your goal of millionaire in a shorter time frame. As an example, this year you can contribute a maximum of $15,000 per year into a Roth 401K.

If you contribute $15,000 per year and make 10% return you would accumulate your $1,000,000 in approximately 20 years.

If you contribute $15,000 per year and make 15% return you would accumulate your $1,000,000 in approximately 16 years.

I want to point out a little known secret. This strategy applies to anyone who has time to watch their investments grow. You can utilize this strategy for yourself or as a way to accumulate a nest egg for your children or grandchildren (who you employ through your business). You will be better off the sooner you start contributing to your retirement account. Even a one time investment of $2,000 which grows at 15% per year will be worth $1,000,000 in approximately 41 years!

Investment Example #4

If you just contributed $2,000 for each of five years and then never put another dime into your retirement account it would accumulate to $1,000,000 approximately 25 years after your last contribution if you received a 15% per year return on your money.

Investment Example #5

If you just contributed $4,000 for each of five years and then never put another dime into your retirement account it would accumulate to $1,000,000 approximately 22 years after your last contribution if you received a 15% per year return on your money.

That is the beauty of compound value of money, the eighth wonder of the world. You are better off contributing for a few years early in life and then just letting your account accumulate than you are to put large amounts into your account year after year when you are older.

Don't forget that your eBay business can make you a millionaire. If your eBay business did nothing more than enable you to convert non-business expenses into legitimate deductions, help subsidize the appreciation of your home and your subsequent net worth, and free up money to contribute to your retirement account to grow tax free, you could easily surpass your dreams and become a millionaire. You could even accomplish this by having an eBay business in addition to your regular job. But by implementing the suggestions throughout this book and through continued use of the ProfitBuilder Software to grow profits, your eBay business could even grow to a million dollar business in its own right. If you get to that point, you would be well on your way to becoming an eBay multi-millionaire.

15

The Final Word

While reading this book you have most likely come to the conclusion that running an eBay business is not a simple task. There are a number of elements that need to come together correctly in order for your business to be successful. The task of launching or revamping an eBay business may seem daunting, but if you start small and build a solid business model from the ground up, you will be just fine.

For new and existing sellers, the first step is to think about your business to determine what type of business you want to be. Do you want to sell retail products with high margins in low volume? You could also have a low-cost, high-volume business model that allows your business to be successful if you sell thousands of products while keeping all costs to an absolute minimum. Another strategy is to focus on liquidated items that you purchase in bulk to offer to customers at closeout prices. Whatever you decide, you need to have a strong understanding of what you want to achieve so you can carve out a clear path to get where you want to go.

If you are an existing seller, the next step is to examine your existing business to identify what areas need improvement. Look at the type of products you sell, the depth of your product line, your conversion rates, profit margins and customer service policies. Some good questions to think about are:

- What are your sales goals, and more importantly, what are your goals for profitability?
- Is there enough demand for the products you are selling to achieve your sales goals?
- Can you expand your product line?
- Are there other products you could offer that would be complementary to your current product line?
- Would it be beneficial to expand your product line?
- Are your profit margins currently where you want them to be?
- Do you even know what your profit margins really are?
- Are you using any software to examine your true profitability and risk?
- Are there any specific products or types of products that are currently costing you more money than they are generating?
- Is your feedback rating as high as you would like it to be? If not, what have customers been dissatisfied with?
- Do your shipping and handling rates and customer service policies promote profitability and customer satisfaction?

- Are your ways of processing customer orders, maintaining inventory and providing customer service as time and cost efficient as they could be?
- Do you consistently have enough supply of products to match the demand you are seeing from your customers?
- If you were an eBay customer in the market for a product you currently sell, would you want to purchase from your business? Or would you choose to buy from a different seller or off of eBay altogether? If so, what could you change to make someone want to purchase from you?
- Is your company registered legally with the government?
- Are you utilizing all the possible tax breaks available to your business?
- Would adding additional employees to your staff enhance or take away from your profitability?
- Are you constantly researching to stay on top of shifts in demand for specific products?
- Are you prepared to handle the increased demand during the holiday season?
- Are you taking full advantage of other seasonal spikes in demand, like Halloween and Valentine's Day?
- How does your business stack up to the competition, both on and off eBay?
- Do you have any ambition to expand your business to other sales channels beyond eBay?
- Are you taking all of the possible tax deductions available to you as a business owner?
- Are you investing a portion of your profits into retirement accounts to grow your net worth to millionaire status?

These questions are a good starting point to analyze where your business is currently and where it could go if you took full advantage of the opportunities available to you. The world of eBay is constantly changing, and will require a great amount of attention on your part if you want to stay ahead of the pack. Don't make the mistake of thinking your eBay business is something you can eventually walk away from and put on "auto-pilot," at least not if one of your goals is to remain profitable. It is natural for entrepreneurs to eventually pull themselves away from the business to pursue other ventures, but someone as qualified as you will have to take over managing the operations of the company if you wish to pursue something else.

As your business begins to take off try to pace yourself. Growing too fast is a common pitfall that hurts companies not quite prepared for the growth. If you see an explosion in sales and cannot fulfill the orders as quickly and efficiently as you once did you risk a catastrophic blow to your feedback score. This kind of attack on your feedback record can be difficult to recover from and badly hurt your reputation. In addition, your attempt to keep up with this spike in demand may cause you to lose track of what is really happening with your profitability. You need to continue to monitor your conversion rates and unsold listings to make sure the company remains as profitable as it needs to be. Give 100% to your business but take it slow and steady when pushing for additional growth.

I also highly recommend attending eBay Live, no matter what stage you are at with your business. EBay Live will be an important step towards the growth of your business. You will meet other sellers, attend seminars on topics you never even thought about, find solutions to problems you have had with your business and learn about new tools and strategies to take your business to the next plateau. Another benefit of eBay Live that I happen to think is great is the top seller panels which I participated in earlier this year. During these panels you will get to hear several top sellers share their experiences of success with the audience. In addition, most of the session is geared towards questions from the audience. This will allow you to tap into the minds of those who have had immense experience with eBay and growing a business to get some insight into ways of fixing your current problems or new strategies you could implement to make your business more effective. Plus, if you have any specific questions about this book you would like to ask me in person, maybe we will get a chance to chat there.

Before you dive into this business, you need to ask yourself if you are passionate about running an eBay business. Passion is the driving force in our lives. The sellers who are most successful are the ones who love what they do and are excited to wake up in the morning and get to work. Running an eBay business is challenging and time consuming, but can be fun and rewarding if you are passionate about it. If you work hard, manage your time, experiment and explore new ideas each day, you can create the next great eBay business and achieve your goals.

Once you have started this process, it's easy to take tax deductions and to use that money to invest in retirement accounts that will grow to astounding levels. Manage your eBay business carefully, watch your costs and be sure to take some of what you make and put it into retirement accounts, regardless of your age. Following this simple strategy will ensure that you will become the next eBay millionaire!

APPENDIX:

More Profitability And Unsold Listing Examples

Example A-1

Listing format on eBay: Fixed Price

Buy It Now Price:	$9.00
Shipping and handling charged to customer:	<u>$5.00</u>
Total price charged to customer:	$14.00
Cost of goods from supplier:	$8.00
Cost of postage:	$1.52
Cost of packaging materials:	$0.25

Listing upgrades and additional features: none

PayPal rate: 2.9% + $0.30 (based on less than $3,000/month sales volume)

Fees for this example:

EBay insertion fee:	$0.35
EBay Final Value fee:	$0.47
PayPal fee:	$0.71
Total fees:	$1.53

Profitability for this example:

Total amount charged to customer:	$14.00
Cost of goods from supplier:	$8.00
Total fees:	$1.53
Cost of postage:	$1.52
Cost of packaging materials:	$0.25
Net Profit:	**$2.70**

Example A-2 - Fixed Price listing above $24.99 with no additional features

Listing format on eBay: Fixed Price

Buy It Now Price:	$38.00
Shipping and handling charged to customer:	$5.00
Total price charged to customer:	$43.00
Cost of goods from supplier:	$30.00
Cost of postage:	$3.00
Cost of packaging materials:	$0.40

EBay feature fees: none

PayPal rate: 2.9% + $0.30 (based on less than $3,000/month sales volume)

Fees for this example:

EBay insertion fee:	$1.20
EBay Final Value fee:	$1.70
PayPal fee:	$1.55
Total fees:	$4.45

Profitability for this example:

Total amount charged to customer: $43.00

Cost of goods from supplier: $30.00

Total fees: $4.45

Cost of postage: $3.00

Cost of packaging materials: <u>$0.40</u>

Net Profit during 1st listing:	**$5.15**
Net Profit during 2nd listing:	**$5.15**
Net Profit during 3rd listing:	**$2.75**
Net Profit during 4th listing:	**$1.55**
Net Profit during 5th listing:	**$0.35**
Net Profit during 6th listing:	**$-0.85**
Net Profit during 7th listing:	**$-2.05**
Net Profit during 8th listing:	**$-3.25**
Net Profit during 9th listing:	**$-4.45**
Net Profit during 10th listing:	**$-5.65**

With this example we started with a much higher profit margin than we have been working with, simply because we are assuming we were able to achieve a relatively high sales price compared to what the item is costing us to purchase from our supplier. But even so, the high insertion fee of $1.20 diminishes our profitability as we move down the line.

Listing 1: Same as always.

Listing 2: You received an insertion fee credit from eBay so your profit remains the same since there are no additional feature fees.

Listing 3: Now that your item has gone through twice you will not be receiving any insertion fee credits from eBay. You lost your insertion fee on the first and second listing ($1.20 a piece). Therefore, your reductions are as follows:

$1.20
+$1.20
$2.40

Net Profit During 1st Listing:	$5.15
Reduction from unsold listings:	($2.40)
Net Profit During 3rd Listing:	**$2.75**

Listings 4-10: From here on out, you will pay an extra $1.20 insertion fee for each additional time the listing goes through. For listings 4 through 10, profitability has been reduced by

$1.20 each step of the way. By listing #6, you are in the negative, and it gets pretty ugly from there on out.

Example A-3 - Same as Example A-2, but with a gallery picture added

Listing format on eBay: Fixed Price

Buy It Now Price:	$38.00
Shipping and handling charged to customer:	$5.00
Total price charged to customer:	$43.00
Cost of goods from supplier:	$30.00
Cost of postage:	$3.00
Cost of packaging materials:	$0.40

EBay feature fees: none

PayPal rate: 2.9% + $0.30 (based on less than $3,000/month sales volume)

Fees for this example:

EBay insertion fee:	$1.20
EBay gallery fee:	$0.35
EBay Final Value fee:	$1.70
PayPal fee:	$1.55
Total fees:	$4.80

Profitability for this example:

Total amount charged to customer: $43.00

Cost of goods from supplier: $30.00

Total fees: $4.80

Cost of postage: $3.00

Cost of packaging materials: <u>$0.40</u>

Net Profit during 1st listing:	**$4.80**
Net Profit during 2nd listing:	**$4.45**
Net Profit during 3rd listing:	**$1.70**
Net Profit during 4th listing:	**$0.15**
Net Profit during 5th listing:	**$-1.40**
Net Profit during 6th listing:	**$-2.95**
Net Profit during 7th listing:	**$-4.50**
Net Profit during 8th listing:	**$-6.05**
Net Profit during 9th listing:	**$-7.60**
Net Profit during 10th listing:	**$-9.15**

Similar to what was illustrated in example #12, the gallery feature absolutely decimated your profit as the listings continued to go through. If you plan to use this feature, make sure that you are able to create enough interest to sell your item during one of the first few listings.

Listing 1: Same as always.

Listing 2: You received an insertion fee credit from eBay, but you need to subtract the gallery fee that is not refunded ($0.35 each time a listing goes through).

Listing 3: Now that your item has gone through twice, you will not be receiving any insertion fee credits from eBay. You lost your insertion fee on the first and second listing ($1.20 a piece), and the gallery fee ($0.35 each) on each of your first two listings. Therefore, your reductions are as follows:

```
  $1.20
+$1.20
+$0.35
+$0.35
  $3.10
```

Net Profit During 1st Listing:	$4.80
Reduction from unsold listings:	($3.10)
Net Profit During 3rd Listing:	**$1.70**

Listings 4-10: From here on out, you will pay an extra $1.20 insertion fee and a $0.35 gallery fee for each additional time the listing goes through. For listings 4 through 10, profitability has

been reduced by $1.55 each step of the way. By listing #4, you are almost unprofitable (in fact you most likely are because of the hidden costs we talked about) and the number just gets worse and worse from there.

The following is another example of how adding listing upgrades such as the gallery picture can change the rate at which your profits diminish. The example is exactly the same as #14, but with a gallery picture added.

Example A-4 - Higher insertion fees with a gallery picture

Listing format on eBay: Fixed Price

Buy It Now Price:	$55.00
Shipping and handling charged to customer:	$5.00
Total price charged to customer:	$60.00
Cost of goods from supplier:	$45.00
Cost of postage:	$3.00
Cost of packaging materials:	$0.40

EBay feature fees: none

PayPal rate: 2.9% + $0.30 (based on less than $3,000/month sales volume)

Fees for this example:

EBay insertion fee:	$2.40
EBay gallery fee:	$0.35
EBay Final Value fee:	$2.21
PayPal fee:	$2.04
Total fees:	$7.00

Profitability for this example:

Total amount charged to customer: $60.00

Cost of goods from supplier: $45.00

Total fees: $7.00

Cost of postage: $3.00

Cost of packaging materials: $0.40

Net Profit during 1st listing:	**$4.60**
Net Profit during 2nd listing:	**$4.25**
Net Profit during 3rd listing:	**$-0.90**
Net Profit during 4th listing:	**$-3.65**
Net Profit during 5th listing:	**$-6.40**
Net Profit during 6th listing:	**$-9.15**
Net Profit during 7th listing:	**$-11.90**
Net Profit during 8th listing:	**$-14.65**
Net Profit during 9th listing:	**$-17.40**
Net Profit during 10th listing:	**$-20.15**

Listing 1: Same as always.

Listing 2: You received an insertion fee credit from eBay, but you need to subtract the gallery fee ($0.35 each time a listing goes through).

Listing 3: Now that your item has gone through twice, you will not be receiving any insertion fee credits from eBay. You lost your insertion fee on the first and second listing ($2.40 a piece), and the gallery fee ($0.35 each) on each of your first two listings. Therefore, your reductions are as follows:

```
 $2.40
+$2.40
+$0.35
+$0.35
 $5.50
```

Net Profit during 1st Listing:	$4.60
Reduction from unsold listings:	($5.50)
Net Profit during 3rd Listing:	**$-0.90**

Listings 4-10: From here on out, you will pay an extra $2.40 insertion fee and $0.35 gallery fee for each additional time the listing goes through. For listings 4 through 10, profitability has been reduced by $2.75 each step of the way. If your item had to be listed 10 times before it sold you would have lost over $20 on the sale.

Example A-5 - Higher insertion fees with a gallery picture and a subtitle

Listing format on eBay: Fixed Price

Buy It Now Price:	$55.00
Shipping and handling charged to customer:	$5.00
Total price charged to customer:	$60.00
Cost of goods from supplier:	$45.00
Cost of postage:	$3.00
Cost of packaging materials:	$0.40

EBay feature fees: none

PayPal rate: 2.9% + $0.30 (based on less than $3,000/month sales volume)

Fees for this example:

EBay insertion fee:	$2.40
EBay gallery fee:	$0.35
EBay subtitle fee:	$0.50
EBay Final Value fee:	$2.21
PayPal fee:	$2.04
Total fees:	$7.50

Profitability for this example:

Total amount charged to customer: $60.00

Cost of goods from supplier: $45.00

Total fees: $7.50

Cost of postage: $3.00

Cost of packaging materials: <u>$0.40</u>

Net Profit during 1st listing:	**$4.10**
Net Profit during 2nd listing:	**$3.25**
Net Profit during 3rd listing:	**$-2.40**
Net Profit during 4th listing:	**$-5.65**
Net Profit during 5th listing:	**$-8.90**
Net Profit during 6th listing:	**$-12.15**
Net Profit during 7th listing:	**$-15.40**
Net Profit during 8th listing:	**$-18.65**
Net Profit during 9th listing:	**$-21.90**
Net Profit during 10th listing:	**$-25.15**

Listing 1: Same as always.

Listing 2: You received an insertion fee credit from eBay, but you need to subtract the gallery and subtitle fees which are not refunded ($0.35 and $0.50 each time a listing goes through).

Listing 3: Now that your item has gone through twice, you will not be receiving any insertion fee credits from eBay. You lost your insertion fee on the first and second listing ($2.40 a piece), and the gallery and subtitle fee ($0.35 and $0.50 a piece) on each of your first two listings. Therefore, your reductions are as follows:

```
 $2.40
+$2.40
+$0.35
+$0.35
+$0.50
+$0.50
 $6.50
```

Net Profit During 1ˢᵗ Listing:	$4.10
Reduction from unsold listings:	($6.50)
Net Profit During 3ʳᵈ Listing:	**$-2.40**

This is your "make-or-break" point for this item. Even if your item sells this time through, you have already lost money on the sale. Look at the difference in profit between listings 2 and 3; it drops by $5.65! Most of this loss occurs because of the high insertion fee that is lost twice, and a smaller but significant amount of the loss comes from the fees for the subtitle and gallery. If you are going to use all of those features, make sure you can sell your item during one of the first two listings.

Listings 4-10: From here on out, you will pay an extra $2.40 insertion fee, a $0.35 gallery fee and a $0.50 subtitle fee for each additional time the listing goes through. For listings 4 through 10, profitability has been reduced by $3.25 each step of the way. If your item had to be listed 10 times before it sold you would have lost over $25 on the sale.

GLOSSARY

Appreciation – Increase in value of an asset in excess of its cost.

Assets – What a person or business owns.

Auction listings – A 3, 5, 7, or 10 day listing in which bidders compete to win the item.

Automation – Using technology to automatically perform certain tasks.

Bad Debts – Write offs of unrecoverable debt from customers (such as when they agree to purchase but do not pay for an item).

Bid – When a buyer makes an offer to potentially purchase the item if no other buyers offer to purchase at a higher price.

BIN – "Buy It Now" allows buyers to end an auction early by agreeing to purchase the item at a pre-determined price specified by the seller.

"Bottom line" – Refers to the net profitability of a company.

Business deductions – Expenses that can be deducted from total gross business income.

Business expenses – Allowable expenses incurred in the operation of a business.

Business processes – Methods of accomplishing the tasks necessary to run a business.

Business structures – The legal form under which a business operates such as a Sole Proprietorship, Partnership, LLC, S Corporation or C Corporation.

Buy It Now fees – Fees charged by eBay for running an auction that includes a Buy It Now option.

Cash Flow – The flow of money in and out of a business.

Complementary product – A product that is related to another product. For example, an iPod accessory is a complementary product to an iPod.

Compounded return /Compounding – Investment return where interest is paid on previous interest as well as increasing on principal.

Consumer – An individual who purchases products from a retailer.

Conversion rate – The number of sold listings vs. the total number of listings. To calculate the conversion rate, take the number of sold listings and divide it by the total number of listings.

Corporation – Legal form of business considered separate from its owners that provides asset protection.

Cost management – Method of understanding the true costs of doing business, and how to structure these costs in an efficient manner.

Cost of goods – Cost of purchasing products to sell from a supplier.

Distributor – A supplier of wholesale products

Drop-shipping – A method of order fulfillment in which the supplier of an item ships directly to the consumer on behalf of the retailer.

EBay Live – EBay's annual convention and training event.

EDI (Electronic Data Interchange) – A technical way of electronic order transmission allowing a business to transmit their product orders to another company or fulfillment house for the orders to be processed.

Equity – Value of a business in excess of the liabilities against the business.

Feature fees – Listing upgrades offered by eBay to enhance the look and visibility of eBay listings.

Feedback – The system that allows buyers and sellers to leave reviews of their experiences interacting with each other. Feedback is used by buyers to evaluate how trustworthy and efficient a seller might be.

Final value fee – Fee charged by eBay when a listing ends successfully with a buyer who has agreed to purchase the item.

Fixed price listings – A 3, 5, 7 or 10 day listing in which the seller specifies the price at which they would like to sell the item. There is no bidding using this format.

Fulfillment houses – Warehouses that hold inventory for a number of businesses, and "pick, pack and ship" orders for these companies as they come in.

Good til' cancelled – A Store Inventory listing that renews itself automatically every 30 days.

Grace period – A period of time where the retailer does not have to make any payments or pay any interest for recent charges on the account.

Gross revenue – The total dollar amount of all sales or services rendered by a company.

Gross sales – The total dollar amount of all sales made.

Immediate payment – An option available to eBay sellers to require buyers to pay immediately through PayPal to purchase an item.

Insertion fee – Fee charged by eBay for listing an item for sale on www.ebay.com.

Insertion fee credit – A refund given by eBay for the second insertion fee paid if an item does not sell during the first listing, but it re-listed and sold during the second listing.

Limited Liability Company – Legal form of business that provides asset protection and a choice of how to be taxed.

Liquidation – The process of selling off excess items at below-market prices in order to obtain cash quickly.

Liquidator – A supplier of wholesale products that specializes in overstock and closeout items that can be sold at below-market values.

Listing formats – Different methods of listing items for sale on eBay. The three formats are Auction, Fixed Price and Store Inventory listings.

Listing upgrades – Upgrades offered by eBay to improve the appeal and visibility of an eBay listing.

Loss leaders – A popular product that a retailer sells below cost to bring customers into the store. This strategy is used given the assumption that customers will purchase additional products from the company either now or in the future.

Manufacturer – A company that produces products in a factory.

Marketing – Method of advertising your business to consumers.

Market trends – Any time outside factors influence buying behavior. Examples include events such as Christmas, Halloween and the September 11th attacks.

Merchant accounts – An arrangement made with a banking institution that allows sellers to process credit cards payments.

"Money float" – A gap between the time when a retailer receives money from a customer and the time when the retailer must pay the supplier for the products that are purchased.

Multi seller ID strategy – A strategy in which sellers can have multiple eBay seller IDs, allowing them to create a different image (if desired) for each of their IDs.

Negotiating – The process of bargaining with another company to obtain the best pricing and terms.

Net Profit margin – The amount of profit received from a sale after all expenses have been accounted for.

Net worth – Total value of assets minus liabilities.

No reserve – A term used to describe an auction item that will sell no matter how low the final bid is.

Packaging materials – Any material used to package an order for shipment, such as envelopes, boxes and tape.

Partnership – Legal form of business with more than one owner and unincorporated status.

Paypal fee – Fee charged by PayPal for receiving PayPal payments from buyers.

Powerseller – An eBay seller that meets the following criteria:

- Have been an active member for 90 days
- Average a minimum of $1000 in sales per month for three consecutive months
- Achieve an overall Feedback rating of 100 of which 98% or more is positive
- Have an account in good financial standing

Product acquisition – The process of locating and purchasing items for future sale.

Profitability – The amount of money a company retains from revenue after all costs having been deducted.

Profitbuilder Risk Level – A level on a scale of 1 to 5 that identifies how much risk of profit loss an item carries.

Profitbuilder Risk Ratio – A ratio that helps assess the risk of listing an item for sale at a certain price. The ratio is calculated by taking the net profit margin during the first listing and dividing it by the total eBay listing fees for each time the item is listed.

Profitbuilder Software – The patent-pending software program that helps eBay sellers save thousands of dollars by understanding how unsold listings and the use of specific listing features can dramatically impact the profitability of eBay businesses.

Re-listing – When an item goes unsold and is then listed for sale using eBay's re-list feature.

Resale license – Sales tax license issued by the state. Required so you can resell items purchased from suppliers. You would be responsible for collecting and forwarding sales tax to the state.

Retailer – A business that sells products directly to consumers.

Retirement account – Tax advantaged investments to be used at a later date.

Risk management – Method of understanding the risk of profit loss, and how to avoid such losses.

Sales revenue – The total dollar amount of all sales made.

Sales volume – The total dollar amount or quantity of all sales made.

Second chance offer – An eBay feature that allows sellers to offer the same product to a losing bidder at the maximum bid entered by that bidder. This occurs when the seller has extra stock of a product available.

Sole Proprietorship – Legal form of business with one owner and unincorporated status.

Starting bid – The minimum bid for an auction specified by the seller.

Store inventory listing – A Fixed Price listing that has a duration of 30 days or more. These listings have reduced visibility in comparison to Auction and Fixed Price listings.

Supply chain – The source of all products that are sold in a retail market. Usually includes a manufacturer, distributor/supplier, retailer and a consumer.

Sweep account – A special bank account that is similar to a business checking account, but transfers the balance of the account during the night to a different account that earns interest on the balance.

Tax benefit – Enables you to pay less tax.

Tax Bracket – The highest percentage of income tax that you owe based on graduated tax tables.

Tax credits – Dollar for dollar reduction from your tax liability.

Tax deductible business expenses – Expenses that reduce business taxable income.

Tax Deduction – An expense allowed to be deducted from taxable income.

Tax Free – No taxes will be due.

Tax loopholes – Legal government incentives to promote business ownership.

Tax write offs – Amounts deducted from taxable income.

Trade shows – Conventions that showcase many products and services from related industries.

Unpaid items – A situation in which the buyer that has agreed to purchase the item does not pay.

Unsold listings – Items listed for a duration of time on eBay that do not have a winning bidder at the end of the listing period.

INDEX

1 cent listing, 40, 49-52

A

Auctions
  listing format 29, 30, 39-52
  auction with BIN 41-46, 71, 72, 75-82, 86, 88-91
  see also profitability examples
  see also unsold listings, effect on profit
  auction with BIN vs fixed price
  86-91

B

benefits of ebay business 231-235
  home business helps

subsidize
  home appreciation 229, 230
  home office 207, 208, 228
  employee relatives 216, 233
  fund start up costs 210
  lower your tax bill 214, 215,
  219-229, 231
  tax breaks for businesses 213-215, 231

BIN (*see also* Buy It Now)
  fees 26, 27
  fee chart 26, 27
  BIN options 39, 41-48, 71, 88
  bold feature 79-82
boxes 105
boxes from businesses 106

C

awful 190,191
good 188, 189
mediocre 189, 190
dealing with angry
customer 194-196
email 128-130, 194
over promise and over
deliver 193

D

distributors and wholesalers
141, 142, 146, 147
finding distributors 144,
149
distributors that accept
returns 147-148
dropshipping 118 (*also see*
fulfillment houses)

E

ebay live 14, 241
ebay suspension 64
email 128-130, 194
employees 208, 209
employee relatives 216, 233
employee wages 126-128

F

feature fees 27, 28, 69
feedback
build exceptional record
196
leave for customers 196-7
fees
BIN fees 26, 27
feature fees 27, 28, 69
final value fees 25, 26
final value fee credit 25
insertion fees 24, 25, 52,
53, 106, 107
insertion fee credit 69, 73
final value fees 25, 26
final value fee chart 25
final value fee credit 65
paypal fees 28, 115
financing inventory 58-60

fixed price
fixed price listing format
30, 32-39, 83-86, 92-94,
108-111, 243-252
fixed price @ break points
107-111
see also profitability
examples
see also unsold listings,

how to present yourself
143-144
what you want 151-153
what you can get 153-154
questions to ask 154-156

P

packaging materials 104
packaging orders 130-132
paypal fees 28, 115
powersellers 14
priority mail boxes 105
product pricing
  complementary products
  182,183
  different pricing strategies
  177-180
  liquidating 148, 149
  mixed bag pricing 180-182
  undercutting competition
  175-176
product selection 157
  do your research 159-161
  ultra competitive
  categories 157, 158
product risk 161-173
product sources
  distributors 141, 142, 146,
  147

finding distributors 144,
149
finding distributors who
accept returns 147-148
liquidators 145-147
manufacturers 140-142
retailers 141
supply chain 139-142
trade shows 149
profitability examples
overview 31
auction with BIN 41-46,
71-72, 75-82, 86, 88-91
auction without BIN 47-52
auction starting at a penny
49-52
fixed price 32-39, 83-86,
92-94, 108-111, 243-252
store inventory format 60-
64
profitability, strategies to
boost
answering emails 128-130
boxes 105
boxes from businesses 106
business deductions 214-
215, 222-229
cashiers checks and money
orders 120
create new listings to save
fees 113-115

S

T

tax breaks for business 213-215, 231
  business tax deductions 215, 222-229
  government wants you to succeed 213, 231
  home office tax deductions 215, 228, 229
  lower your tax bill 214, 215, 221-229, 231
  personal expenses converted to business expenses 215, 216, 228-230
  special tax loopholes for homeowners 228, 229
  travel deductions 216, 227

U

unpaid items 64-66
unsold listings, effect on profit 67-95
unsold listings examples overview 69, 70
  auction with BIN 71, 72, 75-80
  auction without BIN vs fixed price 86-91

bold feature 79-82
fixed price 108-111, 245-252
fixed price @break points 107-111
gallery feature 75-82, 249-259
higher insertion fees 83-94, 245-259
subtitle feature 256-259

W

wealth building strategies
  home business helps subsidize
  home appreciation 229, 230
  increase tax savings 214-216, 221, 222
  investment examples 232, 234
  investment strategies 233, 234   special investment programs available for business owners 231, 232
  special loopholes for home-owners 228
  take legitimate business deductions 222-229

About the Author

Corey Kossack is the President and Founder of Koss DVD LLC, which sells DVDs, video games and books on eBay and www.kossdvd.com.

He has been designated by eBay as a "Top Seller", a status that is only awarded to the top 200 sellers in all of eBay. In addition, Corey has lectured at eBay's annual convention and training event, eBay Live.

Corey is also the creator of the patent-pending ProfitBuilder Software™, which reveals how sellers can save thousands of dollars by understanding how unsold listings and the use of specific listing features can dramatically impact the profitability of eBay businesses. Using a special risk management formula, the ProfitBuilder Software helps sellers choose the best items to list for sale to effectively manage their risk of profit loss.

Corey has received a number of honors for his entrepreneurial efforts, including the 3rd place winner for the Global Student Entrepreneur Award in the Western region, and has been profiled by publications such as the Arizona Republic.

ProfitBuilderSoftware.com

Save your eBay business thousands of dollars using the ProfitBuilder Software!

- Automatically calculates eBay fees

- Automatically calculates PayPal fees

- Automatically calculates net profit margins for the first 10 attempts to sell the item

- Reveals which listing features and formats yield the most profitability

- Identifies the risk of profit loss for each of your eBay listings using a special risk management formula

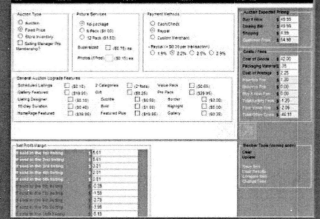

- Helps you choose the listing and pricing strategies that create the most profit for your company

- Helps you decide which items to list for sale

"The best investment you will ever make in your eBay business!"

- Corey Kossack
President
Koss DVD LLC